CITYSPOTS
CARDIFF

Kerry Walker

Written by Kerry Walker
Original photography by Neil Setchfield
Front cover photography © Scott Hortop/Alamy Images
Series design based on an original concept by Studio 183 Limited

Produced by Cambridge Publishing Management Ltd
Project Editor: Rachel Wood
Layout: Trevor Double
Maps: PC Graphics
Reproduced by permission of Ordnance Survey on behalf of HMSO. © Crown
copyright 2006. All rights reserved. Ordnance Survey Licence number 100035725

Published by Thomas Cook Publishing
A division of Thomas Cook Tour Operations Limited
Company Registration No. 1450464 England
PO Box 227, Unit 18, Coningsby Road
Peterborough PE3 8SB, United Kingdom
email: books@thomascook.com
www.thomascookpublishing.com
+ 44 (0) 1733 416477

ISBN-13: 978-1-84157-620-6
ISBN-10: 1-84157-620-4

First edition © 2006 Thomas Cook Publishing
Text © 2006 Thomas Cook Publishing
Maps © 2006 Thomas Cook Publishing
Series Editor: Kelly Anne Pipes
Project Editor: Linda Bass
Production/DTP: Steven Collins

Printed and bound in Spain by GraphyCems

CONTENTS

SYMBOLS & ABBREVIATIONS

The following symbols are used throughout this book:

ⓐ address   ☎ telephone   🖷 fax   ⓔ email   ⓦ website address
🕐 opening times   🚇 public transport connections   ❶ important

The following symbols are used on the maps:

ℹ️ information office		○	city
✈ airport		○	large town
➕ hospital		○	small town
🛡 police station		▬	motorway
🚍 bus station		▬	main road
🚆 train station		▬	minor road
✝ cathedral		—	railway
❶ numbers denote featured cafés & restaurants			

Hotels and restaurants are graded by approximate price as follows:
£ budget   ££ mid-range   £££ expensive

▶ *The picture-perfect Norman keep of Cardiff Castle*

INTRODUCING
Cardiff

Introduction

Europe's cultural Cinderella, Cardiff has brushed aside its industrial image and is looking better than ever. A multi-million pound makeover has transformed the city in recent years, so if you haven't been for a while, you're in for a surprise. A glance at the glittering waterfront development of Cardiff Bay, the mighty Millennium Stadium and iconic Senedd confirms that the Welsh capital has widely embraced change. The intoxicating result is what happens when 2,000 years of history meets the modern world.

With a population of just 317,000, Cardiff is a compact capital by international standards, but it outgrew its small-city boots long ago. The youngest capital in Europe is remarkably diverse, with world-class sights and late nights to rival any of the biggies you care to mention. To complete the picture, top that off with friendly locals, a generous helping of parks, elegant Victorian shopping arcades and lofty castles. Whether you're seeking Monet or Mozart, olde-worlde pubs or funky clubs, cheap backpacker digs or chichi boutique hotels, you're in the right place.

It isn't hard to see what makes the Welsh capital tick: rugby and real ale, comedy and culture, edgy art and avant-garde architecture all add to the appeal of this multifaceted city. A successful blend of the very old and the very new, experience the best of both by climbing Cardiff Castle's Norman keep and sipping latte in a glass-fronted café in Cardiff Bay, wallowing in the civic grandeur of Cathays Park's Edwardian buildings then taking a tour of the futuristic Millennium Stadium.

But the story doesn't end there. Cardiff is simply the introduction to southern Wales. Scratch beneath the surface to find surf, secluded coves and Celtic castles on the Glamorgan Heritage Coast.

Alternatively, venture farther west to the Gower Peninsula for prehistoric caves, standing stones and clean waters. To the north, wild moors and conical peaks make the Brecon Beacons perfect hiking and mountain-biking terrain. So depending on how long you're planning to stay, you can cram a fair bit of the coast and country into a city break to Cardiff.

◗ *A view over the city from Penarth Headland*

When to go

SEASONS & CLIMATE

It's no secret that the weather in Wales is fickle – and Cardiff is no exception. You may find yourself basking in brilliant sunshine one minute, then taking shelter from a heavy downpour the next. But even if the sun doesn't shine, there's no reason to let wet weather put a dampener on your stay. Come well prepared with plenty of layers and waterproofs, particularly if you're planning on hiking and biking the coast or mountains.

May to September is your best bet for fine, sunny weather as temperatures usually hit the 20°Cs (70°Fs). This is the time when the city really comes to life, with open-air concerts, festivals and carnivals two a penny. The warmest months are also great for exploring the secluded coves of the Glamorgan Heritage Coast and Gower, or heading north to climb the peaks of the Brecon Beacons.

While Cardiff is at its wettest during the winter from November to February, temperatures hover around 5°C (41°F) and rarely drop below freezing. This is a good time to visit if you want to beat the crowds and explore the sights in relative peace.

Spring is the season to glimpse the gardens of Roath Park, Bute Park and Cathays Park in bloom, or enjoy long coastal walks as the days get longer and weather milder. Expect temperatures of approximately 10–15°C (50–60°F) from March to May, and a mixed bag of bright sunshine and blustery showers.

ANNUAL EVENTS
February–March
Six Nations Rugby Europe's leading teams battle it out for the title at the Six Nations Championship, a highlight in the Rugby Union

calendar. If you want a piece of the action, you should book tickets well in advance. The event takes place at Cardiff's Millennium Stadium. ⓐ Westgate Street ⓣ 0870 013 8600 (Millennium Stadium) ⓦ www.6nations.net

February–May (biennial)
Artes Mundi Prize Artists from around the world compete for the coveted Artes Mundi Prize. Held every second year (even years), the contemporary visual arts prize pushes the creative boundaries at Cardiff's National Museum & Gallery. ⓐ Cathays Park ⓣ 029 2022 7600 ⓦ www.artesmundi.org

△ *A sunny summer's afternoon in Bute Park*

July

Welsh Proms St David's Hall stages the Welsh Proms, a superb programme of orchestral and jazz highlights. From Brahms to Beethoven, these concerts are a must for classical music enthusiasts. ⓐ The Hayes ❶ 029 2087 8444
Ⓦ www.welshproms.co.uk

July–August

Cardiff Festival This must-see festival takes over Cardiff for two months of open-air concerts, theatre, live music, children's entertainment and funfairs. From carnival beats to food festivals and classical music, this top event pulls out all the stops in summer. ❶ 029 2087 2087 (festival hotline) Ⓦ www.cardiff-festival.com

August

Admiral Cardiff Big Weekend The UK's biggest free outdoor party, the Admiral Cardiff Big Weekend is the grand finale to the summer festival. Live music, funfairs and fireworks draw revellers to the city centre in droves. ❶ 029 2087 2087 (festival hotline) Ⓦ www.cardiff-festival.com

September

Cardiff Mardi Gras This mammoth Mardi Gras is free and takes place in Coopers Field. Thousands flock to Cardiff to celebrate the largest gay party in Wales. ❶ 029 2046 1564 Ⓦ www.cardiffmardigras.co.uk

October

Cardiff Marathon Feet pound Cardiff's streets as the annual marathon comes to town. The race kicks off in Westgate Street and continues to Cardiff Bay and Canton, before returning to the

WHEN TO GO ➡

finishing post at the Millennium Stadium. ☎ 0870 428 6102
ⓦ www.cardiffmarathon.org

November
Cardiff Screen Festival This ten-day festival screens the best of
international cinema. Over 300 screenings and events, from
premières to experimental productions, draw film buffs to venues
across Cardiff. ☎ 029 2030 4400 (ticket hotline)
ⓦ www.cardiffscreenfestival.co.uk

November–December
Winter Wonderland 'Tis the season to get your skates on, as the
gardens in front of City Hall are transformed into an ice rink. Warm
up on the heated terrace, enjoy live music or test out the rides at
the funfair. ⓦ www.cardiffswinterwonderland.com

December
Wales Rally GB Cardiff steps up a gear for the finale of the 16-round
FIA World Rally Championship (WRC). ☎ 029 2023 4509 (ticket
hotline) ⓦ www.walesrallygb.com

NATIONAL PUBLIC HOLIDAYS
New Year's Day 1 Jan
Good Friday Mar/Apr
Easter Monday Mar/Apr
May Day Bank Holiday First Mon May
Spring Bank Holiday Last Mon May
Summer Bank Holiday Last Mon Aug
Christmas Day 25 Dec
Boxing Day 26 Dec

Cardiff Festival

Summer in the Welsh capital spells the Cardiff Festival, a head-spinning mix of late-night parties, live concerts, classical highlights and family events. Headlining the city's summer calendar, this five-week open-air festival in July and August is one of the biggest in the UK. Expect an electric vibe, a fun-loving crowd and an eclectic programme stretching from improvised theatre to funfairs.

The sheer size of the festival means it is split into a number of smaller events, many of which are free. Street entertainment and one-off performances are another big draw.

If you want to swing to soul or sway to salsa, check out the Cardiff Worldport Festival, where folk, Latin and jazz concerts inject musical life into venues across the city. Meanwhile, all the world's a stage at the Museum of Welsh Life at St Fagans. Come here to see thespians take the stage by storm at the Everyman Open Air Theatre Festival, staging Shakespeare classics alongside children's favourites.

How can you keep the kids amused? Take them to Tesco Children's Festival, a weekend of puppet shows and clowns, fairground rides and face painting that takes over Cooper's Field behind Cardiff Castle. At the same time, classical music lovers can hear symphony orchestras, soloists and choirs hit the high notes at the Welsh Proms, held at St David's Hall.

Foodies should make a beeline for Cardiff Bay's International Food & Drink Festival, whetting appetites with world flavours from France, Germany, Italy and Spain, plus flavoursome Welsh fare. While the weekend is given over to jugglers, acrobats and mime at the free International Street Festival.

Flamboyant parades, the sound of steel drums and samba music round out the festival in style, as the multicultural MAS Carnival comes to Cardiff Bay. This builds up to the big finale: the three-day Admiral Cardiff Big Weekend, featuring live music, a huge funfair and fireworks each night. With a line-up like this, it's no surprise that people come back year-in year-out.

For more information contact ☏ 029 2087 2087
ⓦ www.cardiff-festival.com

🔺 *Family fun – with lobsters – at the Cardiff Festival*

History

Although Cardiff's roots can be traced back as far as 600 BC when the Celts invaded Europe, the city was first established when the Romans built a fort here in AD 75. This is the site where Cardiff Castle now stands, sheltering over 2,000 years of Welsh history.

Following centuries of Viking, Norman and Irish invasions, a key turning point in Cardiff's history took place in the 16th century. In 1542, Thomas Capper was burned at the stake for heresy, then hailed Wales' first religious martyr. That same year the second Act of Union was introduced, which divided Wales into shires, established a new justice system and made English the official language of Wales. From then on, Welsh speakers were banned from holding public office. This bone of contention sparked an age-old conflict between England and Wales that still bubbles under the surface today.

In 1658, Cardiff was back on the map when Welsh participation in the English Civil War culminated in the Battle of St Fagans with heavy losses. To this day, battle reenactments take place at St Fagans National History Museum where these historic events unfolded.

Cardiff prospered, industry flourished and the population spiralled during the 19th century, when the Marquis of Bute opened

THE WELSH NOT

The Welsh language is an integral part of Cardiff's identity, so it's hard to believe that little more than 150 years ago people were punished for uttering a single word in Welsh. At school, children were forced to speak English and those that dared to converse in Welsh were beaten or forced to wear the loathed 'Welsh Not', a wooden necklace that was a mark of shame.

Cardiff's first dock in 1839 and the first rail link was built in 1845 linking Cardiff to nearby coal-producing valleys.

The wealth that coal mining and iron smelting brought during the Industrial Revolution meant that Cardiff grew steadily. It was finally granted city status in 1905, and was famous at that time as the world's biggest coal exporter.

The coal industry gradually declined and the face of the city changed – Welsh was made the official language in 1942 and Cardiff became the capital of Wales in 1955. Like most of South Wales, Cardiff suffered greatly when industry in the region collapsed. However, this vibrant university city has successfully propelled itself into the 21st century, boasting the stunning new waterfront development of Cardiff Bay and more parks per square mile than any other UK city. Cardiff is now out of the dark and looking forwards to a brilliant future.

⬤ *A statue in Cardiff Bay recalls the city's proud mining heritage*

Lifestyle

Modern and buzzing, Cardiff has 26,000 students, making it Europe's youngest capital. Perhaps the real secret of this Welsh beauty lies in its scale – small enough to get around easily, yet big enough to feel like a city. Or maybe it's because Cardiff remains rooted to its heritage, despite the multi-million pound regeneration projects that have revamped the city.

The people from Cardiff are irrefutably Welsh and proud of it, showing growing confidence and a strong sense of national identity. While the vast majority speak English as their first language, they don't like to be called British, or worse still English. Impress the locals by dropping a few words of Welsh into the conversation. Although Cardiff has been Anglicised, more people still speak Welsh than any other surviving Celtic tongue.

Down to earth and friendly, the locals are a charismatic bunch that like to sing (as the city's high proportion of choirs shows) and love to laugh. Cardiff is, in fact, the UK's comedy capital. Witticisms, quips and banter always go down well with a pint of locally brewed Brains bitter.

Aware of their tradition but by no means traditional, Cardiff's residents are a young, party-loving lot that like to play as hard as they work, as a night out in the trendy bars along Cardiff Bay or in the city centre's lively pubs and clubs confirms.

While song and laughter are close to Cardiff's heart, the capital has only one true passion: rugby. Love it or loathe it, the locals live and breathe this rough and rugged sport, with local team the Cardiff Blues enjoying a huge following. Join the fans to soak up the sports-mad atmosphere in the Millennium Stadium.

▶ *Enjoying a drink on the waterfront at Cardiff Bay*

Culture

Sassy, bold and ever-evolving, today's Cardiff has got cultural clout, rising out of the industrial ashes as a multicultural and multilingual city. With a thriving arts and music scene, the city is currently making waves with edgy art galleries, world-class auditoriums and well-preserved Victorian buildings. These qualities helped the city make the shortlist of the 2008 European Capital of Culture.

Whether you prefer opera greats or pints down the local, Cardiff hits the spot. A thriving student population and pioneering urban regeneration projects like Cardiff Bay have made the jewel in the Welsh crown glitter once again. From strings and sopranos at St David's Hall to Impressionist watercolours at the National Museum & Gallery, Cardiff is a magnet to culture vultures.

The first stop for music lovers should be St David's Hall, a 2,000-seat venue offering some of the best acoustics in Europe, which hosts the Welsh Proms in summer and the biennial Cardiff Singer of the World Competition. Another must is the glittering slate-and-glass Millennium Centre in Cardiff Bay, where the Welsh National Opera perform. This is also the place to catch everything from West End musicals to rock concerts.

Avid theatregoers should book tickets for the turn-of-the-century New Theatre, one of Wales' leading performing arts venues that welcomes big names to the stage including the Royal National Theatre. For quirky adaptations, try the Sherman Theatre. The Chapter Arts Centre presents thought-provoking productions in one of Europe's largest cultural venues.

▶ *The Millennium Centre is the home of the Welsh National Opera*

ST FAGANS NATIONAL HISTORY MUSEUM

Six km (4 miles) west of Cardiff, the open-air St Fagans National History Museum explores 500 years of Welsh history and heritage in the 40-hectare (100-acre) grounds of 16th-century St Fagans Castle. Displays and craft workshops are held in 40 traditional buildings including a school, chapel and Workmens' Institute. Step inside to see the galleries exhibiting Welsh costume and farming implements. Native breeds of livestock roam the paddocks and farmyards, and demonstrations of traditional farming tasks take place daily.

🔹 St Fagans ☎ 029 2057 3500 🌐 www.museumwales.ac.uk 🕐 10.00–17.00

If you're into art, get your fix for free at Cardiff's National Museum & Gallery, showcasing the biggest collection of French Impressionist paintings outside of Paris. Works on display range from old masters like Rubens and Van Dyck to contemporary sculpture. Off the beaten tourist track, the capital is punctuated with smaller, more intimate galleries. Make for the Albany Gallery and Martin Tinney Gallery to enjoy modern Welsh art, and G38 for cutting-edge exhibitions.

With culture at its core, it's little wonder that Cardiff has given rise to some of the music, literary and art world's biggest names. Among them are the virtuoso soprano Charlotte Church, best-selling authors Roald Dahl and Ken Follett, actor Griff Rhys Jones, and bands the Manic Street Preachers and Super Furry Animals. The city that inspired these stars beckons.

▶ *Mermaid Quay on the waterfront at Cardiff Bay*

✓ MAKING THE MOST OF
Cardiff

Shopping

WHERE TO SHOP

Whether you're seeking funky designer labels or antique shops oozing musty charm, markets with local flavour or big high-street names, Cardiff comes up with the goods. Most shops and department stores cluster around central St Mary Street, High Street, Castle Street, Duke Street and Queen Street.

Victorian arcades The city centre is liberally criss-crossed with pedestrianised Victorian arcades, housing everything from one-off boutiques to bookshops and laid-back cafés where you can rest your feet after a morning's speed shop. For the latest trends, make for the split-level Castle Arcade, one of the city's oldest.

Shopping malls Home to chains like Debenhams, M&S and bhs, St David's Shopping Centre on Queen Street is a good choice if it rains or you want to shop under one roof. Next door, the glass-fronted Capitol Shopping Centre draws shoppers to high-street giants like H&M and Virgin Megastores.

Markets Crammed with fresh produce from creamy Welsh cheeses to organic coffee, Cardiff's Victorian Central Market opens 08.00–17.30 Monday to Saturday. You'll also find second-hand books, specialist records, jewellery, local crafts and leather goods. On Sunday morning, sniff out local specialities such as hot Welsh cakes, honey and organic lamb at the Riverside Real Food Market in Cardiff Bay.

▶ *The elegant split-level Castle Arcade*

Eating & drinking

Once upon a time Cardiff's culinary endeavours may have been limited to laverbread (see page 26), leeks and Welsh lamb. But those days are long gone, as the forward-thinking, multi-ethnic capital moves into new gastro waters. OK, so you'll still find Welsh staples on the menu if you want them, but with a modern twist and an emphasis on organic, locally sourced produce.

World flavours also make an appearance, with a mind-boggling array of restaurants, bistros and cafés serving everything from 5-star French cuisine to fiery Bengali curries and sushi on a conveyor belt. So whether your idea of heaven is a spicy samosa in a central curry house or fresh fish in Cardiff Bay's seafood restaurants, you won't go hungry here. The good news is that eating out is still affordable compared to other big cities – pleasing for the stomach and the pocket!

DINING DISTRICTS

Mingle with Cardiff's hip crowd on the buzzing waterfront, the place to come for the freshest seafood and sweeping views. Smart restaurants and bars jostle for your attention around Mermaid Quay, from trendy fish restaurants to Italian trattorias. In summer, it's a great spot for alfresco dining on the terrace.

RESTAURANT CATEGORIES

The restaurant price guides used in this book indicate the approximate cost of a three-course meal for one person, excluding drinks, at the time of writing.

£ = up to £20   ££ = £20–£35   £££ = above £35

You can pretty much eat your way around the world in Cardiff.
For brilliant baltis and cheap-and-cheerful Chinese or Indian buffets,
make a beeline for Albany Road, City Road and Clifton Street in
Roath, one of the capital's main student districts. In the city centre
and Cathays, you'll find everything from Thai restaurants and
Greek tavernas to trendy New York-style delis and Japanese
noodle bars.

Hungry students and clubbers find late-night, post-party food in
City Road, Albany Road, Whitchurch Road and High Street. The fast-
food outlets here selling burgers, kebabs, pizzas, standard Chinese

◐ *Late-night tapas in Cardiff Bay*

fare and fish 'n' chips might not exactly be gourmet, but they serve their purpose with cheap and filling food.

FOOD MARKETS

Every Sunday, the Riverside Market on the Taff Embankment tempts foodies with a mouthwatering selection of fresh, local produce. The perfect pre-picnic shop, here you can fill your bags with Gower cockles, Caerphilly cheese, laverbread (see below) and creamy Welsh fudge. It's best to get there before 13.00, when the stalls start to sell out. From Monday to Saturday, Cardiff's Central Market has a selection of organic fruit and vegetables, Welsh cheeses, seafood, fresh bread and cakes.

WHAT'S THE PALAVER ABOUT LAVER?

Traditionally served with cockles and bacon, laverbread (or *bara lawr*) is a staple of the hearty Welsh breakfast. Edible seaweed may not seem all that appetising, but most locals beg to differ. Hence the fact that this pungent, nutritious speciality appears on many menus. An acquired taste perhaps?

PICNIC SPOTS

Cardiff has plenty of parks and gardens where, weather permitting, you can enjoy a leisurely picnic. Lay your blanket by the lake in leafy Roath Park and tuck into Welsh specialities. Another popular choice is centrally located Bute Park beside Cardiff Castle, where picnickers can laze by the River Taff's banks. A few miles out of town, the Edwardian Dyffryn Gardens are a lovely spot for a picnic on a summer's day. Further afield, the Glamorgan Heritage Coast and Gower's secluded bays are ideal if you're seeking moreish views and peace.

LOCAL SPECIALITIES

Cardiff whets appetites with wholesome, hearty dishes using tasty, simple ingredients. Savour specialities like Welsh rarebit (cheese on toast made with ale), laverbread, tender Welsh lamb and fruity bara brith tea loaf. Warming on damp, dreary days are *crempog* (pancakes with salty Welsh butter) and cawl (a filling stew made with bacon, mutton and leek). There are some flavoursome local cheeses to try including soft Abergavenny goat's cheese, pungent Granston Blue and tangy Caerphilly cheese. Cardiff's proximity to the coast means that fresh seafood is a staple, with restaurants serving everything from cockles to beer-battered cod.

The tipple of choice in Cardiff is beer, such as the locally brewed Brains varieties. Head to one of the city's many pubs to drink pints of amber-coloured Brains Bitter with a sweet-malt flavour, Brains Dark ale or hoppy Brains SA with a bitter-sweet finish and fruit note. Nearby vineyards also produce wines and grape-based spirits. Refreshing alternatives are hand-pressed cider, elderflower drinks and perry (a fermented pear beverage).

Entertainment & nightlife

Home to some of the UK's leading performing arts venues, more pubs and clubs than you can shake a stick at, plus a student population that just wants to have fun, Cardiff rocks by night.

🔺 *A hot summer's night at the Terra Nova bar (see page 88)*

Moving from pints in a friendly watering hole in Cathays to cocktails in the chichi bars dotting Cardiff Bay and late-night clubbing in the city centre, you're practically guaranteed a good night out here.

Locals tend to hit the pubs and bars early (around 20.00). Although the UK introduced 24-hour drinking laws in 2005, punters still have to drink up by 23.00 in many of the smaller pubs in Cardiff's residential areas and outskirts. Central pubs tend to stay open slightly later and the majority of clubs pump out tunes until around 03.00 at weekends.

Culture vultures are well catered for with a plethora of theatres, concert halls and cinemas – from strings and sopranos at St David's Hall to ballet and opera at the Millennium Centre. If you want to book tickets for a performance, you'll often get the best deal by contacting the venue direct. Alternatively, Ticket Line sells tickets for concerts, sporting events and musicals (ⓐ 47 Westgate Street ⓣ 029 2023 0130 ⓦ www.ticketlineuk.com).

PUBS & BARS

Wall-to-wall pubs and bars vie for custom in central Cardiff around St Mary Street and Mill Lane. A mixture of spit-and-sawdust pubs, trendy bars and everything in-between, this is the place to come if you like your music loud, crowd young and vibe buzzing. Cathays pulls the crowds with a cocktail of funky bars, laid-back pubs and relaxed beer gardens.

A relative newcomer to the Welsh capital's nightlife scene is Cardiff Bay, with a string of sleek bars overlooking the illuminated waterfront. Wood floors, floor-to-ceiling glass and minimalist chic set the scene here. The offer is varied, stretching from live bands at The Point to comedy acts at The Glee Club on Mermaid Quay.

CLUBS

Night owls head for clubs in central Cardiff to dance till the wee hours. St Mary Street is a safe bet for after-dark fun, with top addresses including the Lava Lounge, Life & Liquid, Soda and Toucan. Most open every night of the week.

PERFORMING ARTS

Culture comes in high doses in Cardiff. The modern Millennium Centre hosts world-class opera, dance and ballet productions, and is home to the Welsh National Opera. Not to be outdone, St David's Hall (the National Concert Hall of Wales) is a must for serious music buffs, hosting a superb range of live concerts and free exhibitions.

If theatre appeals, the Sherman Theatre and Chapter Arts Centre beckon; the latter also shows art-house and foreign-language films (most with English subtitles), and is among the venues that play host to the Cardiff Screen Festival in November. Blockbuster movies grace the 12 giant screens at the UCI Cinema in the Red Dragon Centre.

ENTERTAINMENT LISTINGS

The following websites feature information about entertainment and nightlife in Cardiff, plus up-to-date listings of events taking place in the city:

Arts 4 Cardiff Find out what's on at the weekend with this online listing for the arts in Cardiff. The site is updated daily and features the latest details on concerts, theatre, exhibitions and opera. Ⓦ www.arts4cardiff.co.uk

Cardiff Online A comprehensive online guide to Cardiff gigs, theatre, comedy and film screenings. Ⓦ www.cardiffonline.net

My Cardiff Plan a big night out on the town with this informative site listing gigs and concerts, as well as reviews of bars, pubs and clubs. ⓦ www.mycardiff.net

🔵 *St David's Hall is the place to go for serious music-lovers*

Sport & relaxation

SPECTATOR SPORTS

Cardiff has got sport on the brain. If the locals aren't practising on the pitch, you'll find them cheering on their team down the pub or raising the roof when the Blues (a local rugby team) play at home. The rule of thumb is that if there isn't a ball (round, oval or otherwise), it isn't worth watching. Hence the three big spectator sports are rugby, football and cricket.

ⓘ Tickets to see top matches at the Millennium Stadium are like gold dust, so book well in advance. Failing that, join a lively crowd in front of the big screen at The Yard in the Old Brewery Quarter.

PARTICIPATION SPORTS

Hiking Wales is made for walking, so bring some sturdy boots and tackle the coastal paths spanning the Glamorgan Heritage Coast and the Gower Peninsula. Serious trekkers take on the 89-km (55-mile) Taff Trail linking Cardiff to Brecon. **ⓦ** www.tafftrail.org.uk

Mountain biking The downhill rush, the uphill climb ... the beautiful Brecon Beacons beckon mountain bikers, with challenging terrain and spectacular views that make all the sweating worthwhile. **ⓦ** www.mtbbreconbeacons.co.uk

Swimming The biggest bath is the Bristol Channel lapping the coast, but you'd have to be brave to take a dip out of season. Cardiff also has plenty of good indoor options such as the Eastern Leisure Centre, with a pool, gym and sauna.
ⓐ Llanrummney **ⓣ** 029 2079 6616

Watersports Surfing and kite surfing are all the rage on the Glamorgan Heritage Coast. Some of the best waves hit the beaches of Porthcawl and Dunraven Bay near Southerndown. Further west on the Gower Peninsula, adrenaline junkies test out everything from skiing and wake-boarding to kayaking and coast-steering.

If you'd prefer to stay central, Cardiff Bay Water Activity Centre runs supervised sessions for novices and pros. Try your hand at canoeing, bell boating, raft building or jet skiing.

ⓐ Channel View ⓣ 029 2037 8161

RELAXATION

Spa If you want to splash out on the ultimate spa experience, there's only one place to do it. St David's Day Spa offers an arm-long list of therapies. Beauty comes at a cost, but the views of Cardiff Bay from the relaxation lounge are simply priceless.

ⓐ Havannah Street ⓣ 029 2045 4045 ⓦ www.thestdavidshotel.com

🔺 Hikers on the Taff Trail in the Brecon Beacons

Accommodation

From chic boutique suites to country retreats, cheap digs to spa hotels, Cardiff offers a mind-boggling array of accommodation to suit every pocket. If you're on a tight budget, there are a number of decent hostels and guesthouses just a short bus ride away from the centre; many include breakfast in the room rate. If money is no object, splash out on a grand Victorian hotel in the city centre to be at the heart of the action, or choose a contemporary suite with a view of Cardiff Bay.

PRICE RATING
The ratings below indicate the approximate cost of a room for two people for one night.
£ = under £40   ££ = £40–£70   £££ above £70

BED & BREAKFAST

Acorn Lodge £ A good cheapie, this intimate B&B is bright and clean. Cosy rooms have a TV and tea-making facilities, and the friendly owners are more than happy to help. A 15-minute walk from the centre, the small guesthouse has a pretty garden and the breakfast comes recommended. ⓐ 182 Cathedral Road ⓣ 029 2022 1373

Albany Guest House £ Put your feet up at this home away from home. This inviting guesthouse offers snug rooms with tea-making facilities and TV. Buses shuttle travellers into the nearby city centre and breakfasts are substantial. Wheelchair accessible. ⓐ 191–193 Albany Road ⓣ 029 2049 4121

Austin's £ The rooms won't win any design awards, but are spotless. This little red-brick guesthouse overlooks the River Taff and is just a few steps from the castle. Awarded 2 stars by the Wales Tourist Board, it's basic but good value. ⓐ 11 Coldstream Terrace ⓣ 029 2037 7148 ⓦ www.hotelcardiff.com

Beaufort Guest House ££ This high-ceilinged Victorian townhouse has elegant en-suite rooms in creams and blues. Expect a warm welcome and delicious Welsh breakfast. ⓐ 65 Cathedral Road ⓣ 029 2023 7003 ⓦ www.beauforthousecardiff.co.uk

Gelynis Farm B&B ££ This 16th-century stone cottage in the heart of green countryside is just 8 km (5 miles) from Cardiff (a 10-minute train ride). Near Castell Coch, the farmhouse has its own fruit farm and is a great base for those that want to walk the Taff Trail. ⓐ Morganstown ⓣ 029 2084 4440 ⓦ www.gelynisfarm.co.uk

The Laurels ££ A real find is this dreamy, white-washed cottage in St Fagans. With easy access to the M4, this low-key, family-run hotel offers cosy rooms and has village charm. Buses run frequently to the city centre. ⓐ 1 The Laurels, Cardiff Road ⓣ 029 2056 6668 ⓦ www.beechwoodonline.co.uk

HOTELS
Penrhys Hotel ££ This central, family run hotel is set in a well-maintained Victorian house. En-suite rooms are modern and comfortable. Enjoy breakfast beneath the antlers in the eccentric dining room. ⓐ 127 Cathedral Road ⓣ 029 2023 0548 ⓕ 029 2066 6344 ⓦ www.penrhyshotel.com

The Big Sleep Hotel ££ Looking for a room with a view? This place is for you. With its funky retro design, this ultra-cool hotel is one of Cardiff's tallest, affording sweeping views over the city and bay. Glam yet affordable, the converted 1960s block offers sleek rooms and efficient service. ⓐ Bute Terrace ⓣ 029 2063 6363 ⓦ www.thebigsleephotel.com

Wynford Hotel ££–£££ Sports-mad visitors stay in this hotel to be close to the Millennium Stadium. Awarded 2 stars by the Welsh

● *Great views and retro styling at The Big Sleep Hotel*

Tourist Board, this is a cheery place with value-for-money rooms and WiFi access. There's a nightclub, bar and bistro on site. ⓐ Clare Street ⓣ 029 2037 1983 ⓕ 029 2034 0477 ⓦ www.wynfordhotel.com

Angel Hotel £££ Very posh sums up this elegant hotel. Rooms don't come cheap, but if polished marble floors, sweeping staircases and crystal chandeliers are your idea of decadence, you're in the right place. On Cardiff Castle's doorstep, the hotel has WiFi and 24-hour room service. ⓐ Castle Street ⓣ 029 2064 9200 ⓕ 029 2039 6212 ⓦ www.paramount-hotels.co.uk

Cardiff Marriott £££ Part of the Marriott chain, this hotel has a great location in Cardiff's trendy café quarter. Facilities include a spa, gym, sauna and restaurant, while the modern rooms have cable TV, Internet access and minibar. ⓐ Mill Lane ⓣ 0870 4007 290 ⓕ 0870 4007 390 ⓦ www.marriotthotels.co.uk

Jolyons Boutique Hotel £££ Opposite the Millennium Centre, this intimate boutique hotel has six sumptuous rooms. Sink into your king-sized bed, or choose a room with a whirlpool and views of Cardiff Bay. Relax with a coffee by the wood-burning stove in the contemporary bar. ⓐ 5 Bute Crescent ⓣ 029 2048 8775 ⓦ www.jolyons.co.uk

Old Post Office £££ Dine and sleep in style at this contemporary hotel in St Fagans. Light-filled rooms offer simple sophistication, clean contours and plump beds. Foodies flock to the restaurant where award-winning chef Wesley Hammond cooks up a storm. ⓐ Greenwood Lane ⓣ 029 2056 5400 ⓦ www.old-post-office.com

St David's Hotel & Spa £££ The town's most talked about hotel needs little introduction. Guests can enjoy views of Cardiff Bay from their private balconies, dine in the award-winning Tides Grill and steam in the hydrotherapy spa. It might be pricey, but it's pure, unashamed indulgence. ⓐ Havannah Street ⓣ 029 2045 4045 ⓕ 029 2048 7056 ⓦ www.thestdavidshotel.com

◔ Top-of-the-range accommodation at St David's Hotel & Spa

CAMPSITES

Cardiff Caravan Park £ This small, well-kept site scores points for its central location. Bute Park is within arm's reach and the city centre is a 15-minute walk away. The 93 pitches are spacious, showers hot and facilities clean. Open year round, the site has a laundry, resident warden and cycle hire. ⓐ Pontcanna Fields ⓣ 029 2039 8362

HOSTELS

Nos da Inns @ Cardiff Backpackers £ The best budget deal in town is this central, laid-back hostel in a luminous yellow-and-purple building. A five-minute walk from the station, dorms and private rooms are clean and bedding is provided. Facilities feature Internet access, secure lockers, a communal kitchen and bar. A hearty Welsh breakfast is included in the price. ⓐ 98 Neville Street ⓣ 029 2034 5577 ⓦ www.cardiffbackpacker.com

Nos da Inns @ The Riverbank £ The riverside relative of Cardiff Backpackers is being revamped as the Hilton of the hostel world. Backpackers and families can expect en-suite, no-frills rooms. There are left-luggage facilities, a 24-hour check-in, travel desk and nightclub. The barbecue area is popular in summer. ⓐ 53–59 Despenser Street ⓣ 029 2037 8866 ⓦ www.cardiffbackpacker.com

YHA Cardiff £ Cheap digs can be found at this attractive red-brick hostel near Roath Park. Dorms are basic but clean, and there's a lounge and kitchen for guest use. Internet access and lockers are available. Unless you're a YHA member, you'll have to pay a surcharge. ⓐ 2 Wedal Road ⓣ 0870 770 5750 ⓦ www.yha.org.uk

THE BEST OF CARDIFF

TOP 10 ATTRACTIONS

- **Millennium Stadium** Rugby raises pulses at this iconic landmark in the centre – the ultra-modern face of the new city (see page 63).

- **Cardiff Castle** Disney couldn't have done a better job with the turrets and towers of this picture-perfect castle in central Cardiff (see page 60).

- **Techniquest** Scintillating science is the focus of this hands-on discovery museum and planetarium in Cardiff Bay (see page 81).

- **National Museum & Gallery** This is the place to come if you want to admire Monet and van Gogh, Celtic coins and cannon balls all under one roof (see page 95).

- **Llandaff Cathedral** Set in Cardiff's leafy Llandaff district, this cathedral houses Sir Jacob Epstein's eye-catching *Christ in Majesty* statue (see page 63).

- **St David's Hall** High notes reverberate at the National Concert Hall of Wales, as world-class soloists and orchestras take the stage by storm (see page 67).

- **St Fagans National History Museum** Dip into the rich pot of Welsh history and heritage at this free open-air museum, set in the 41-hectare (100-acre) grounds of 16th-century St Fagans Castle (see page 45).

- **Dyffryn Gardens** Cardiff has got a few surprises up its green sleeve and this Grade I listed Edwardian garden is one of them. (see page 106).

- **Senedd** A marvel of modern art and energy efficiency, the National Assembly for Wales dominates Cardiff Bay with its smooth contours and wave-shaped roof (see page 80).

- **Roath Park** Pinned at the city's green heart, this central park has kept its Victorian feel and is the perfect place to escape the crowds (see page 64).

Treorchy Male Voice Choir in front of the Opera House

Here's a brief guide to seeing and experiencing the best of Cardiff, depending on the time you have available.

HALF-DAY: CARDIFF IN A HURRY

Kick off your whirlwind stay in Cardiff Bay, walking along the waterfront to spy the slate-and-steel Millennium Centre, red-brick Pierhead and striking Senedd, plus a string of contemporary sculptures. Following a quick caffeine fix at Mermaid Quay, hop aboard a Cardiff Cat (see page 55) to soak up more sights from the water and reach the city centre.

1 DAY: TIME TO SEE A LITTLE MORE

If you're staying the day, it would be rude not to take a peek behind Cardiff Castle's sturdy doors – climb the Norman keep for the best views. Nearby, take a behind-the-scenes tour of the iconic

● *A tranquil view of Cardiff Bay*

Millennium Stadium or speed shop in Queen's Arcade. Nip into the indoor market and leave with a bag full of Welsh goodies.

2–3 DAYS: SHORT CITY-BREAK

You've seen the stadium, climbed the castle and now you want more? Head to Cathays Park, where fountains and marble statues glam up City Hall. Next up is the National Museum & Gallery , where you can wallow in art and Wales' natural history.

Weather permitting, pack up a picnic and make for Roath Park to relax in the rose gardens, or central Bute Park to laze beside the snaking River Taff. An afternoon is also well spent exploring the open-air St Fagans National History Museum. As night falls, see stars through glass windows in Mermaid Quay's avant-garde bars or on the stage at St David's Hall.

Those with itchy feet can venture further afield to Llandaff Cathedral, home to the controversial *Christ in Majesty* statue, or classic Welsh beauty Castell Coch (Red Castle) tucked away in the hills – all silvery turrets, round towers and vaulted ceilings, it's classic fairy tale stuff.

LONGER: ENJOYING CARDIFF TO THE FULL

Travellers with time on their hands can sample all Cardiff has to offer and then some. Go west to kayak or kite surf on the 23-km (14-mile) Glamorgan Heritage Coast, studded with sheer cliffs and sheltered coves. The unspoilt Gower Peninsula hides secluded bays, caves and its fair share of fossils.

North of Cardiff, Caerphilly sits in the shadow of a castle with a leaning tower to rival Pisa's. Meanwhile, hikers don walking boots to scale the peaks of the Brecon Beacons and hard hats to descend into the mine at Big Pit National Coal Museum.

Something for nothing

The best things in Cardiff are free, so you'll be glad to know you don't have to splurge to enjoy all this city has to offer. Take in a free exhibition (or two) in the top museums and galleries, sculpture-hop your way along futuristic Cardiff Bay, lose yourself in a warren of Victorian buildings in Cathays Park, or simply chill in the capital's parks and gardens. Come in summer for a non-stop line-up of free concerts, parties and parades at the Cardiff Festival.

Millennium Centre

It won't cost you a penny to catch one of the Millennium Centre's free lunchtime, afternoon or early evening performances. The iconic venue in Cardiff Bay stages everything from a cappella choirs to classical, jazz and world music.

🅐 Bute Place 🅘 Box office: 08700 40 2000 🅦 www.wmc.org.uk

🅛 Most free performances begin at 13.00, 15.00 and 18.00

🔺 *Enjoy a free performance at the Millennium Centre*

SOMETHING FOR NOTHING

National Museum & Gallery

One bite isn't enough at this huge museum. From geology to
marine biodiversity, art to archaeology, here you can marvel at
Impressionist masterpieces and shipwrecks, or trace the country's
geology back 700 million years at the Evolution of Wales.
ⓐ Cathays Park ⓣ 029 2039 7951 ⓕ 029 2057 3321
ⓦ www.nmgw.ac.uk ⓛ 10.00–17.00 Tues–Sun, closed Mon

Roath Park

A stroll in this central park blows away the cobwebs. There are rose
and dahlia gardens, subtropical greenhouses and wildfowl,
including cormorants, roosting on the lake's islands. Spot the
lighthouse that pays tribute to Captain Scott.
ⓐ Lake Road West ⓣ 029 2022 7281 ⓛ Open daily

St David's Hall

This leading cultural venue regularly stages free exhibitions, plus
contemporary and traditional craft displays by some of Wales' finest
makers and designers in the Hall's Foyer Galleries. ⓐ The Hayes
ⓣ 029 2087 8444 ⓦ www.stdavidshallcardiff.co.uk ⓛ 10.00–16.00
Mon–Sat, closed Sun

St Fagans National History Museum

Discover Welsh history and heritage at this free open-air museum,
set in the 41-hectare (100-acre) grounds of 16th-century St Fagans
Castle. Farming demonstrations and craft workshops take visitors
back 500 years in time. If you don't have the time, energy or will to
tackle the Taff Trail, the 8-km (5-mile) St Fagans Walk starts here.
ⓐ St Fagans ⓣ 029 2057 3500 ⓦ www.museumwales.ac.uk
ⓛ 10.00–17.00

When it rains

The savvy locals have never let a bit of drizzle from the valleys get them down, so why should you? Cardiff cleverly compensates for Wales' heavy downpours and all-too-spontaneous showers with a host of undercover attractions.

The city's central labyrinth of Victorian arcades and crystalline malls are a great place to take shelter, whether you're trying on the latest high-street trends in the Capitol Shopping Centre, or nipping into the boutiques lining Queens Arcade. Even Cardiff's Central Market is indoors, where you can soak up the lively atmosphere and sniff out local produce. Little wonder then that when Wales rains, Cardiff shops.

Discover Cardiff Bay's top indoor attractions, starting with Wales' political engine the Senedd.

Kids in tow? Take them to Techniquest, an interactive science museum where they can push, pull and prod to their heart's content.

If all that sightseeing has worked up an appetite, warm up with a latte and panini at Coffee Mania (ⓐ Mermaid Quay ① 029 2046 4546 🕐 10.30–20.00).

Those seeking free culture should head for City Hall in Cathays Park. Carved from white Portland stone, the impressive building houses Joseph Farquharson's Winter art collection. The headline attraction, though, is the Marble Hall on the second floor, where marble statues of Welsh heroes like Boudicca and St David vie for your attention.

Nearby is the National Museum & Gallery, where you can brush up against Impressionist masterpieces. Highlights include Monet's *Waterlilies* and a version of Rodin's famous bronze statue *The Kiss*. As well as art, the museum has intriguing displays on biodiversity, geology, archaeology and industry. The eclectic mix of permanent collections and cutting-edge exhibitions provides more than enough entertainment on a damp afternoon.

Ahhh ... the pub, a fine institution that relieves the dull patches of a Welsh winter and Cardiff is no exception. Real ale on tap, squashy leather chairs and a roaring fire are the perfect antidotes to rainy weather. Just around the corner from the museum on Park Grove, that's exactly what you'll find at the oak-panelled Pen & Wig (ⓣ 029 2064 9091 ⓛ 10.00–midnight Mon–Fri, 10.00–01.00 Sat & Sun).

⬥ *Check out the local produce at the Central Market*

On arrival

TIME DIFFERENCES

Cardiff's clocks follow Greenwich Mean Time (GMT). During Daylight Saving Time (end Mar–end Oct) the clocks are put forward one hour. In the Welsh summer when it is 12 noon in Cardiff, the time elsewhere is as follows:

Australia Eastern Standard Time 21.00, Central Standard Time 20.30, Western Standard Time 19.00

New Zealand 23.00

South Africa 12.00

USA and Canada Newfoundland Time 08.30, Atlantic Canada Time 08.00, Eastern Time 07.00, Central Time 06.00, Mountain Time 05.00, Pacific Time 04.00, Alaska 03.00

ARRIVING

By air

Many international airlines serve Cardiff International Airport (ⓐ Rhoose ⓣ 01446 711111 ⓦ www.cwlfly.com), 19 km (12 miles) west of the city centre, flying direct to major destinations across the UK and Europe such as Paris, Brussels, Prague and Amsterdam, plus Vancouver and Toronto in Canada. For budget deals, your best bet is bmibaby, operating a frequent service to a number of key European destinations including Belfast, Glasgow, Faro and Alicante. Other big airlines serving the city include KLM, Excel and Thomsonfly.

Cardiff's compact and modern airport offers a range of facilities. You'll find free luggage trolleys and a tourist information centre in the arrivals hall, a bureau de change on the first floor and an ATM in the departures lounge. There is a food village where you can grab a snack on the run, plus a number of shops for last-minute gifts.

The airport has good public transport connections to the city centre. Trains run every hour between the airport and Cardiff Central station, with onward connections to other destinations. Buy tickets on board the trains from Cardiff International Airport or at the train station ticket desk at Cardiff Central. The Airbus Xpress service X91 operates half hourly between Cardiff and the airport on weekdays and hourly at weekends. A taxi from the airport to the city centre should cost around £25.

By rail

Trains pull into the heart of the city at Cardiff Central, Wales' largest railway station (ⓐ Central Square ⓣ 0845 6061 660). First Great Western (ⓣ 08457 000 125 ⓦ www.firstgreatwestern.co.uk) operates an hourly service to London Paddington; the journey takes roughly

ⓐ All signs in Cardiff, like this one at the station, are in both Welsh and English

2 hours. There are frequent services to other major hubs including Bristol (45 minutes), Swansea (1 hour) and Birmingham (2 hours). National Rail (Ⓦ www.nationalrail.co.uk) gives comprehensive information on fares, destinations and timetables.

You'll find payphones, toilets and ATMs at the station. The concourse has a café, bookshop and newsagents stocking international press. You can book tickets in advance at the station or order them online. Travel is slightly cheaper off-peak (outside of rush hour Monday to Friday and at weekends).

By bus

Cardiff's bus station, in Wood Street, is located close to the Central Station. National Express (Ⓣ 08705 808080 Ⓦ www.nationalexpress.com) stops at rank A and serves destinations including London, Bristol, Oxford and Glasgow. Journey times are longer than by train, but fares are cheaper. A budget alternative is Megabus (Ⓣ 0900 160 0900 Ⓦ www.megabus.com), linking Cardiff to Central London.

Driving

The M4 links Cardiff to other UK cities. From London, the motorway passes Bath and Bristol, before crossing the Severn Bridge that connects England to Wales. Make sure you've got some spare change handy for the toll. Pay-and-display car parks include Castle Mews, Sophia Gardens, and The Barrage in Cardiff Bay. For long-stay parking, head for North Road.

FINDING YOUR FEET

Laid-back, friendly and unpretentious, Cardiff doesn't present many challenges for travellers fresh off the plane. Perhaps this relaxed vibe has something to do with the youthful student population or the high concentration of green spaces providing respite from the city's buzz. Most people that arrive here soon get to grips with the sights and pace of the Welsh capital.

Another plus point for those keen to explore on foot is the pedestrianised city centre around Queen Street and the warren of Victorian arcades. Not having to dodge traffic makes walking a pleasure and takes the stress out of shopping.

❶ As long as you have your wits about you, it's unlikely you'll experience any problems during your stay. Cardiff has a fairly low crime rate, but the general rules apply about not carrying large sums of money, or drawing unwanted attention with expensive jewellery and cameras.

ORIENTATION

Located in South Wales, Cardiff sits on the mouth of the Severn spilling into the Bristol Channel. To the north lie the rolling green hills of the Valleys and Brecon Beacons, to the west the wild Glamorgan Heritage Coast and Gower, and to the east the English–Welsh border.

Cardiff is easy to navigate, with most of the key sights clustering in the centre, where you'll spy Cardiff Castle's towers and the almighty Millennium Stadium. Follow Bute Street 1.6 km (1 mile) south to reach the regenerated waterfront area of Cardiff Bay, or step north to Cathays Park where white Portland stone buildings catch your eye.

Streets fanning out from the centre lead to Cardiff's other districts, including Roath (the student area), Heath (home to the University Hospital of Wales), Llandaff (dominated by a Norman cathedral) and St Fagans (famous for its National History Museum). All are within an 8-km (5-mile) radius of the centre.

Cardiff

0	1000 metres
0	1000 yards

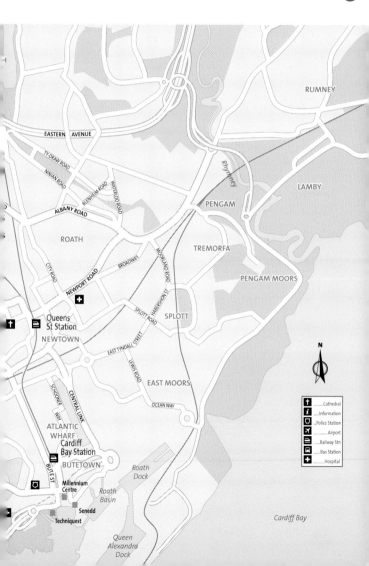

GETTING AROUND

On foot

With pedestrianised shopping streets and most major attractions huddling in the compact city centre, Cardiff is made for walking.

❶ If you're planning on exploring areas off the beaten tourist track, invest in the indispensable *Cardiff A–Z* street map (available at major bookshops).

By bicycle

A bike is a great way to reach the parts cars can't and feet won't. Taff Trail Cycle Hire at the Cardiff Caravan Park hires out high-quality mountain bikes, as well as a range of tandems and trikes.

ⓐ Pontcanna Fields **☎** 029 2039 8362

By bus

Cardiff Bus operates a frequent service in and around Cardiff. You'll need the right change to buy tickets on board. For information on timetables, contact Enquiries **☎** 029 2066 6444

ⓦ www.cardiffbus.com

❶ Save money with a 24-hour CityRider pass, offering unlimited travel on all bus routes.

By train

A local rail network criss-crosses Cardiff, stopping at stations such as Queen Street, Cardiff Bay, Cathays and Llandaff. Cardiff Central links the capital to regional, national and international destinations.

By boat

A laid-back way to see the sights is aboard a Cardiff Cat. These waterbuses sail between The Barrage and Mermaid Quay, and Mermaid Quay and the city centre. Single fares cost around £2; return £4. Boats depart roughly every hour. Ⓦ www.cardiffcats.com

By taxi

Around 400 licensed taxis ply Cardiff's city centre 24/7. There are ranks at Central Station and St David's Hall or you can hail a cab

⬥ *Get a great view of Cardiff Bay from one of the city's waterbuses*

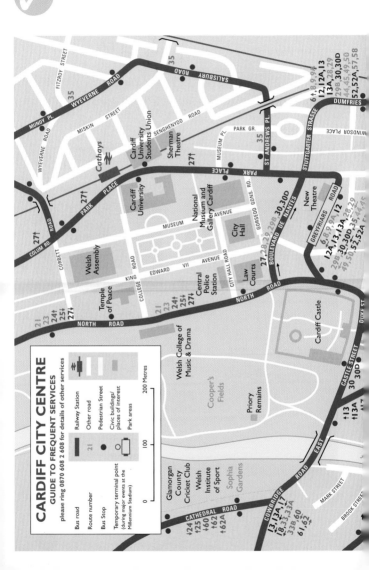

CARDIFF CITY CENTRE
GUIDE TO FREQUENT SERVICES
please ring 0870 608 2 608 for details of other services

Bus road
Route number 21
Bus Stop
Temporary terminal point
(during major events at the
Millennium Stadium)

Railway Station
Other road
Pedestrian Street
Civic buildings/
places of interest
Park areas

0   100   200 Metres

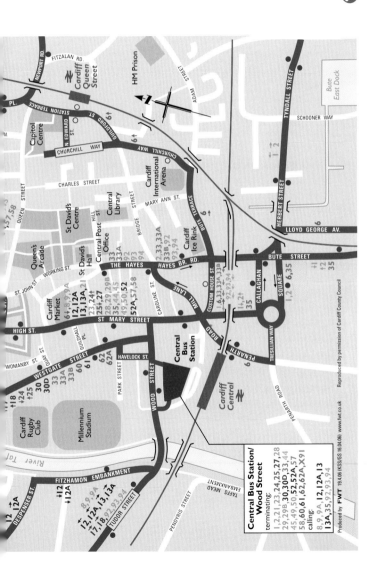

Central Bus Station/
Wood Street
terminating:
1,2,21,23,24,25,27,28
29,29B,30,30D,33,44
45,49,50,52,52A,57
58,60,61,62,62A,X91
calling:
8,9,9A,12,12A,13
13A,35,92,93,94

Reproduced by permission of Cardiff County Council

Produced by FWT 19.4.06 (KSS/GS 16.04.06) www.fwt.co.uk

from the street. All taxis display signs and are equipped with a meter. Expect to pay around £4–£8 for a 5–10-minute journey.

CAR HIRE

Driving in Cardiff is not as daunting as in some capitals, but you're unlikely to need a car if you're planning to spend most of your time in the city centre. Cardiff is so compact that walking or getting around by public transport is easy and hassle-free. If you want to explore the nearby coast, valleys and mountains, having your own set of wheels is a good (but by no means the only) option. All the major car-rental agencies (including those listed below) are represented in Cardiff, either in the centre or in the short-stay car park opposite the terminal at the airport.

Avis ⓐ 14–22 Tudor Street ⓣ 029 2034 2111 ⓦ www.avis.co.uk
ⓛ 08.00–18.00 Mon–Fri, 08.00–13.00 Sat, closed Sun
Budget ⓐ Penarth Road ⓣ 029 2022 3131 ⓦ www.budget.co.uk
ⓛ 08.00–18.00 Mon–Fri, 08.00–13.00 Sat, closed Sun
Europcar ⓐ At the airport ⓣ 01446 711924 ⓦ www.europcar.co.uk
ⓛ 08.00–21.30 Mon–Fri, 09.00–16.00 Sat, 13.00–21.00 Sun
Hertz ⓐ 9 Central Square ⓣ 029 2022 4548 ⓦ www.hertz.co.uk
ⓛ 08.00–17.30 Mon–Fri, 09.00–12.00 Sat, closed Sun
National Alamo ⓐ At the airport ⓣ 01446 719528
ⓦ www.alamo.com ⓛ 08.00–21.30 Mon–Fri, 08.00–14.00 Sat, 13.30–21.30 Sun
Sixt ⓐ 356 Newport Road ⓣ 08701 567 567 ⓦ www.e-sixt.co.uk
ⓛ 07.30–18.00 Mon–Fri, 08.00–12.00 Sat & Sun

▶ *A proud Welsh dragon at Cardiff International Arena*

THE CITY OF
Cardiff

Cardiff City Centre

Sandwiched between Cathays and Cardiff Bay, the compact city centre lies at Cardiff's geographical core and is a curious blend of old and new, from the almighty Millennium Stadium to Cardiff Castle's stone towers and wistful turrets. Interwoven with elegant Victorian arcades and punctuated with leafy parks and modern malls, the central hub does trendy, traditional and everything in-between. After dark, The Old Brewery Quarter is the place to party till the wee hours.

SIGHTS & ATTRACTIONS

Bute Park
This pretty park is a splash of greenery on the urban landscape. A magnet for city workers and students, this huge open space is flanked by the River Taff, Sophia Gardens, Pontcanna Fields and Cardiff Castle. Come here to chill on the river banks and stroll the flower gardens.
ⓐ Western Avenue ❶ 029 2068 4000 ◷ Open daily

Cardiff Castle
Disney couldn't have done a better job with the turrets and towers of this picture-perfect castle. Sitting on 2,000 years of history, the castle has Roman roots but the keep is Norman. Step inside to admire the elaborate rooms decorated with stained glass, murals and marble.
ⓐ Castle Street ❶ 029 2087 8100 ⓦ www.cardiffcastle.com
◷ 09.30–18.00 (summer); 09.00–17.00 (winter). Admission charge

Cardiff Metropolitan Cathedral of St David
Just off Queen Street, this imposing cathedral was built in 1887 to accommodate 12,000 Catholics fleeing famine in Ireland. Following

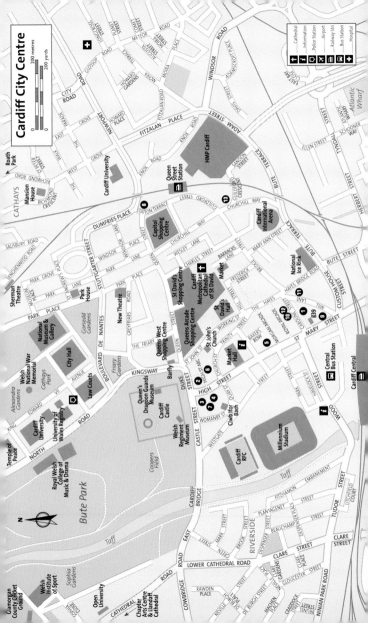

extensive bombing during World War II, it was rebuilt brick by brick.
ⓐ 38 Charles Street ⓣ 029 2022 7281 ⓛ Open daily

City Sightseeing Bus

Hop on at Cardiff Castle, put your feet up and let the red bus whisk
you off on a head-spinning 50-minute tour, taking in the National
Museum & Gallery, Millennium Stadium and Cardiff Bay.
ⓣ 029 2038 4291 ⓦ www.guidefriday.com ⓛ Buses depart every
30 minutes. Admission charge

Llandaff Cathedral

Set in Cardiff's leafy Llandaff district, this cathedral is one of Britain's
oldest Christian sites, dating back to the 6th century. Inside, Sir
Jacob Epstein's modern aluminium statue *Christ in Majesty* stands
in striking contrast to the Gothic arches. It's well worth the 15-
minute ride from the city centre.
ⓐ Cathedral Road ⓣ 029 2056 4554 ⓦ www.llandaffcathedral.org.uk
ⓛ Open daily ⓦ Buses 24 and 33

Millennium Stadium

This iconic landmark is the face of the new city. Home to the Welsh
Rugby Union, the concrete-and-steel giant is a marvel of modern
technology with a fully retractable roof. Since hosting the Rugby
World Cup in 1999, Europe's largest covered stadium has staged a
string of world-class sporting events and concerts. Take a peek
behind the scenes with a stadium tour.
ⓐ Westgate Street ⓣ 0870 013 8600 ⓦ www.millenniumstadium.
com ⓛ 10.00–17.00 Mon–Sat, 10.00–16.00 Sun. Admission charge

◐ *Climb up to* Castel Caerdydd, *or Cardiff Castle*

Roath Park

The perfect place to escape the crowds, this central park has kept its Victorian feel. Highlights feature the subtropical greenhouse, rose and dahlia gardens, plus the lake's islands that are a haven for wildlife like cormorants. The lighthouse pays tribute to Captain Scott, whose voyage to the Antarctic began in Cardiff.

ⓐ Lake Road West ⓣ 029 2022 7281 ⓛ Open daily

Sophia Gardens

The city's first public park, Sophia Gardens opened in 1858. Today the grounds are home to the Glamorgan County Cricket Club.

ⓐ Cathedral Road ⓣ 029 2040 9380 ⓦ www.ecb.co.uk ⓛ Open daily

St John's Church

Seek solace from the city's buzzing shopping district at this medieval church. Sitting on the same spot for over 800 years, St John's takes pride of place among Cardiff's oldest buildings and was rebuilt in the perpendicular style in the 15th century. See the light hit the slender stained-glass windows. Peace at last!

ⓐ St John's Square ⓣ 029 2022 0375 ⓦ www.cardiffcentralparish.org ⓛ 10.00–16.00 Mon–Sat, hours of worship Sun

CULTURE

Barfly

Up-and-coming talent, budding new stars … Hot, loud and sweaty, this venue is one of the best in Cardiff for live music.

ⓐ Kingsway ⓣ 0870 907 0999 ⓦ www.barflyclub.com ⓛ Open daily

▶ *An oasis of calm – St John's Church*

Cardiff International Arena

This vast arena is the life and soul of central Cardiff. From West End musicals to major concerts, top comedy acts to major sporting events, the action is here.

🅐 Mary Ann Street 🕿 029 2022 4488 Ⓦ www.cclive.co.uk/cia
🕒 Open daily

Chapter Arts Centre

Just to the west of Cardiff in Canton, this dynamic arts centre houses a cinema, theatre and gallery. Emphasis is on the unconventional, from physical theatre to thought-provoking plays.

🅐 Market Road 🕿 029 2030 4400 Ⓦ www.chapter.org 🕒 Box office: 11.00–20.30 Mon–Fri, 14.00–20.30 Sat, 15.00–20.30 Sun Ⓝ Buses 17, 18 and 31 leave Cardiff Central every 5 minutes

Clwb Ifor Bach

Speak a little Welsh? Cardiff's Welsh-language club is the place to immerse yourself in the local language and culture, and enjoy live music from rock to retro. Non-members are usually welcome, but it's worth checking on the club's noticeboard in advance.

🅐 11 Womanby Street 🕿 029 2023 2199 Ⓦ www.clwb.net
🕒 Open daily

g39

From the cutting edge to the downright controversial, this funky little gallery stages temporary exhibitions by up-and-coming Welsh artists. Expect a mix of contemporary photography, video and sculpture.

🅐 Wyndham Arcade, Mill Lane 🕿 029 2025 5541 Ⓦ www.g39.org
🕒 11.00–17.30 Wed–Sat, closed Sun–Tues

St David's Hall

High notes reverberate at the National Concert Hall of Wales, where world-class soloists and orchestras make an entrance. As well as hosting the Welsh Proms, Cardiff's key cultural venue stages dance productions and concerts, plus free exhibitions in the gallery foyer. ⓐ The Hayes ⓣ 029 2087 8444 ⓦ www.stdavidshallcardiff.co.uk ⓛ Open daily

RETAIL THERAPY

Buzz & Co Treat your feet to a pair of ultra-cool shoes. ⓐ 13 High Street Arcade ⓣ 029 2038 2149 ⓛ 10.00–17.30 Mon–Sat, closed Sun

Capitol Shopping Centre This glass-fronted shopping mall on Queen Street is a one-stop shop for high-street names like H&M, Oasis and Swatch. ⓐ Queen Street ⓣ 029 2022 3683 ⓦ www.capitol-shopping-centre.co.uk ⓛ 08.30–18.00 Mon–Sat, 11.00–17.00 Sun

Castle Galleries Buy original paintings, limited-edition prints, sculpture and ceramics by contemporary artists at this gallery. ⓐ Queen Street ⓣ 029 2022 2020 ⓦ www.castlegalleries.com ⓛ 08.30–18.00 Mon–Sat, 11.00–17.00 Sun

Castle Welsh Crafts Looking for a lovespoon or a Celtic cross? Pick up Welsh souvenirs at this shop opposite the castle. ⓐ 1 Castle Street ⓣ 029 2034 3038 ⓛ 09.00–17.30 Mon–Sat, 10.00–16.00 Sun

Central Market Fresh cockles and sugary Welsh cakes tempt shoppers at Cardiff's indoor market, housed in a Victorian building. ⓐ The Hayes ⓣ 029 2087 1214 ⓛ 08.00–17.30 Mon–Sat, closed Sun

🔺 *Very nice shops in the elegant Victorian High Street Arcade*

Gentlefolk The denim is to die for at this ultra-trendy shop, selling every kind of jeans imaginable. ⓐ 30–32 Castle Arcade ⓣ 029 2023 2344 ⓛ 10.00–17.00 Mon–Sat, closed Sun

Nice Shop Spacey lamps, quirky kitchen gadgets, and weird and wonderful gifts at this interior design shop. ⓐ 12–14 High Street Arcade ⓣ 029 2064 5181 ⓦ www.nicespace.co.uk ⓛ 10.00–17.30 Mon–Sat, 12.00–16.00 Sun

Pussy Galore Looking for funky clubwear and gorgeous gowns? This is the place. ⓐ 18 High Street Arcade ⓣ 029 2031 2400 ⓛ 10.00–17.30 Mon–Sat, closed Sun

Queens Arcade Big high-street shops like Argos and Next mix with smart boutiques and speciality shops here. ⓐ Queen Street

☎ 029 2022 3581 ⓦ www.queensarcade.info 🕐 09.00–17.30
Mon–Sat, 11.00–17.00 Sun

Spillers Records Go to vinyl heaven at the world's oldest record shop,
founded in 1894. ⓐ 36 The Hayes ☎ 029 2022 4905
ⓦ www.spillersrecords.co.uk 🕐 09.30–17.45 Mon–Sat,
11.30–16.00 Sun

St David's Centre Make a beeline for this shopping centre, home to
department store giants like Debenhams and M&S. ⓐ Queen Street
☎ 029 2039 6041 🕐 08.30–18.30 Mon–Wed, 08.30–20.00 Thur–Sat,
11.00–17.00 Sun

Woodies Emporium From Paul Smith to Pringle, designer labels line
the shelves in this chic store. ⓐ 22–26 Morgan Arcade ☎ 029 2023
2171 ⓦ www.woodiesemporium.com 🕐 09.00–17.30 Mon–Thur,
09.00–18.00 Fri & Sat, closed Sun

TAKING A BREAK

Ask £ ❶ Bright, modern and buzzy, this restaurant is the perfect
pizza pit stop. Sit on the terrace when the sun shines. ⓐ 24–32
Wyndham Arcade, Mill Lane ☎ 029 2034 4665 🕐 12.00–23.00
Sun–Thur, 12.00–23.30 Fri & Sat

Bella Italia £ ❷ This no-frills chain restaurant serves
inexpensive antipasti, pasta and pizza. Check out the special
lunch menus. ⓐ 6 High Street ☎ 029 2038 7185
ⓦ www.bellapasta.co.uk 🕐 11.30–22.30 Mon–Thur, 11.30–23.00
Fri & Sat, 12.00–22.00 Sun

Café Minuet £ ❸   This little café is a real find. Enjoy authentic Italian fare just like mama used to make and perhaps the finest cappuccino in town. ⓐ 42 Castle Arcade ⓣ 029 2034 1794 ⓛ 11.00–16.00 Mon–Sat, closed Sun

Celtic Cauldron £ ❹   A welcome break from the centre's throngs, this snug restaurant opposite the castle scores top points for flavoursome dishes like Welsh rarebit and laverbread. ⓐ 47–49 Castle Arcade ⓣ 029 2038 7185 ⓛ 08.30–18.30 Mon–Fri, 08.00–18.00 Sat, 11.00–16.00 Sun

Louis Restaurant £ ❺   Fill up on good-value home-made food at this laid-back restaurant. Generous portions and cheery staff make this a good choice for breakfast or lunch. ⓐ 32 St Mary Street ⓣ 029 2022 5722 ⓛ 09.00–19.45 Mon–Sat, 10.00–16.30 Sun

New York Deli £ ❻   The sandwiches at this deli are enormous and the bagels take some beating too. ⓐ 18 High Street Arcade ⓣ 029 2038 8388 ⓛ 09.00–17.00 Mon–Sat, closed Sun

The Organic Juice Co £ ❼   Freshly pressed, vitamin-rich juices pack a punch. Health-conscious locals come here to eat organic soups or grab a mango smoothie. ⓐ 18 Castle Arcade ⓣ 029 2038 8778 ⓦ www.theorganicjuiceco.co.uk ⓛ 10.00–18.00 Mon–Sat, closed Sun

Zushi £ ❽   Eat sushi and surf the web at this funky Japanese noodle bar. Choose whatever takes your fancy from the colour-coded dishes on the conveyor belt. ⓐ 140 Queen Street ⓣ 029 2066 9911 ⓦ www.zushicardiff.com ⓛ 12.00–22.00 Mon–Sat, 12.00–17.00 Sun

---

❿ *Cardiff's Millennium Stadium*

AFTER DARK

Restaurants

Champers £ ❾ The crowd is young, colours warm and the vibe buzzy at this popular Spanish restaurant in the centre. This is the place to eat home-made tapas in Cardiff with a nice bottle of Rioja. ⓐ 60–62 St Mary Street ❶ 029 2039 8036 ⓦ www.le-monde.co.uk/champers.htm ❶ 11.30–23.30

Chiquito £ ❿ Sizzling fajitas and tequila on tap are on the menu at this cheery Mexican chain. The atmosphere is relaxed and child-friendly. ⓐ The Old Brewery Quarter ❶ 029 2038 7465 ⓦ www.chiquito.co.uk ❶ 12.00–23.00 Mon–Sat, 12.00–22.30 Sun

Las Iguanas £ ⓫ Brazilian lime chicken and potent Caipirinha cocktails make this prime party territory. Go Latino here with a group of friends and dine before dancing downstairs. ⓐ 9 Mill Lane ❶ 029 2022 6373 ⓦ www.iguanas.co.uk ❶ 12.00–23.00 Mon–Thur, 12.00–23.30 Fri & Sat, 12.00–22.30 Sun

Spice Quarter £ ⓬ Tangy massalas and fiery vindaloos whet appetites at this sleek and central Indian restaurant. Vegetarian menus are available. ⓐ The Old Brewery Quarter ❶ 029 2022 0075 ⓦ www.spicequarter.co.uk ❶ 12.00–14.30, 17.00–23.00

The Thai House Restaurant ££ ⓭ Spicy curries and steaming noodles tempt hungry travellers at this award-winning Thai restaurant opposite the CIA. Ingredients are fresh, service efficient and the wine list impressive. ⓐ 3–5 Guildford Crescent ❶ 029 2038 7404 ⓦ www.thaihouse.biz ❶ 12.00–15.30, 18.30–23.00 Mon–Sat, closed Sun

Bars & clubs

Café Jazz Sounds of the sax liven up this laid-back venue, staging top-quality jazz and blues gigs most nights. ⓐ 21 St Mary Street ⓣ 029 2023 2161 ⓛ 11.30–23.30

Copa This relaxed and central bar is quiet enough to converse and serves continental beers, including cherry-flavoured Kriek beer from Belgium. ⓐ 4 Wharton Street ⓣ 029 2022 2114 ⓛ 11.30–23.00 Mon–Wed, 11.30–midnight Thur, 11.30–01.00 Fri & Sat, 12.00–22.30 Sun

Floyd's Bar Blink and you might miss this tiny bar, popular among Cardiff's hip crowd. Dark wooden floors, leather sofas and soul music set the scene. The cocktails are excellent and the vibe positively chilled. ⓐ 23 High Street ⓣ 029 2022 2181 ⓛ 19.30–03.00 Thur–Sat, closed Sun–Wed

Jumpin' Jaks Kitsch but fun, this lively place is a refreshing change to the city's trendy bars. From giggling girlies on a hen night to local lads having a ball, come here if you want to let your hair down and bop to chart hits. ⓐ Millennium Plaza, Wood Street ⓣ 029 2034 0737 ⓦ www.jumpinjaks.com ⓛ 19.00–02.00 Tues–Sun, closed Mon

Lava Lounge Try a zesty Lava Cooler at this real life Club Tropicana. This buzzy, retro-style bar plays everything from jazz to classroom classics. ⓐ The Old Brewery Quarter, St Mary Street ⓣ 029 2038 2313 ⓦ www.lavalounge.co.uk ⓛ 11.00–02.00 Wed–Sat, 11.00–01.00 Sun–Tues

Life & Liquid For late-night partying, head to this central club with DJs and live acts. Music moves from funky house to dance anthems.

Entry is free most weeknights. ⓐ St Mary Street ⓣ 029 2064 5464
ⓦ www.liquid-online.com ⓛ 21.30–03.00 Thur, 21.00–02.30 Fri,
21.30–03.00 Sat, 19.00–01.00 Sun–Wed

Moloko More than 60 varieties of vodka fuel clubbers at this trendy,
three-level bar in Cardiff's café quarter. The décor is retro, with glam
touches like leather sofas. Music ranges from drum & bass beats to
disco grooves. ⓐ 7 Mill Lane ⓣ 029 2022 5592 ⓦ www.moloko.info
ⓛ 20.00–02.00 Mon–Wed, 20.00–03.00 Thur–Sat, 20.00–
midnight Sun

Prince of Wales Enjoy a swift pint and spiral staircases at this
Weatherspoon's pub set in an old theatre. ⓐ 82 St Mary Street
ⓣ 029 2064 4449 ⓛ 11.00–23.00 Mon–Sat, 12.00–22.30 Sun

Soda This trendy bar does urban chic well, with cave-like cubby
holes, exposed brick and a black-and-white colour scheme.
It's where Cardiff's hip crowd hang out at night. ⓐ 41 St Mary
Street ⓣ 029 2023 8181 ⓦ www.thesodabar.com
ⓛ 22.00–02.00 Thur, 22.00–03.00 Fri, 22.00–03.30 Sat,
closed Sun–Wed

The Toucan Salsa and sultry jazz breathe life into this bright and
modern bar, decked out in murals and luminous motifs. Sway to
Brazilian Funk and acoustic soul, and soak up the mellow vibe.
ⓐ 95–97 St Mary Street ⓣ 029 2037 2212 ⓦ www.toucanclub.co.uk
ⓛ 12.00–02.00 Tues–Sat, 18.00–00.30 Sun, closed Mon

The Yard The offspring of Brains Brewery, this huge bar has
industrial décor, with exposed brickwork, stainless steel and plasma

screens. It serves Brains bitters and ales, plus value-for-money food.

🅐 42–43 St Mary Street 🅣 029 2022 7577 🅛 10.00–01.00

Union Cardiff Students flock here like thirsty bees to a honey pot.
Set in the Capitol Shopping Centre, this union club plays a good mix
of music, and drinks don't come much cheaper in these parts.

🅐 3 Churchill Way 🅣 029 2064 1010 🅦 www.unioncardiff.com
🅛 19.00–02.00 Wed, 21.00–02.00 Thur, closed Fri–Tues

🔺 *Sample the local brew, Brain's beer, at The Yard*

Cardiff Bay

Seeing the Water Tower glint, the Millennium Centre rise proud and the trendy glass-walled bars lining Mermaid Quay, it's hard to believe that Cardiff Bay was ever the coal-exporting hub it once was. But this Tiger is burning bright again, thanks to a multi-million pound makeover. Welcome to modern Cardiff, a place of cutting-edge architecture, buzzy cocktail bars and ever-so-posh boutiques. Yet scratch beneath the surface and you'll find that the past is still very much alive.

⬤ *Start your visit at 'The Tube', the Cardiff Bay Visitor Centre*

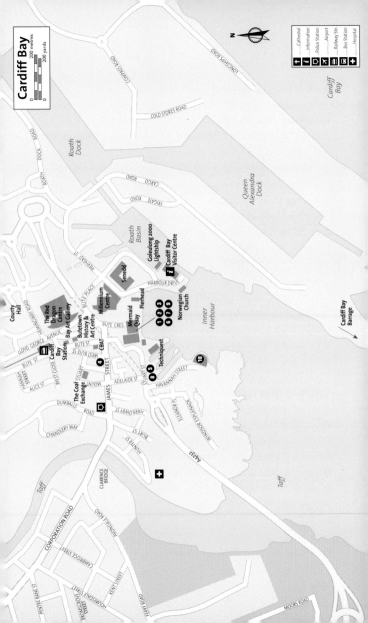

Cardiff Bay

200 metres
200 yards

N

Cathedral
Information
Police Station
Airport
Railway Stn
Bus Station
Hospital

LONG SHIPS ROAD

QUAYS ROAD

Cardiff Bay

COLD STORES ROAD

Roath Dock

ROATH DOCK ROAD

CARGO ROAD

FRIGATE ROAD

Queen Alexandra Dock

Roath Basin

PIERHEAD ST

Senedd

Goleulong 2000 Lightship

Cardiff Bay Visitor Centre

HARBOUR DRIVE

Millennium Centre

BUTE PLACE

Pierhead

i

County Hall

The Red Dragon Centre

Bay Art Gallery

Butetown History & Art Centre

Mermaid Quay

MERMAID CRES.

Norwegian Church

Inner Harbour

Cardiff Bay Barrage

LLOYD GEORGE AVENUE

BUTE ST

WEST BUTE ST

BUTE ST

1 2 3
1 2 3

Cardiff Bay Station

CBAT

4

Techniquest

Taff

HANNAH STREET

BUTE STREET

WEST CLOSE

ALICE ST

STUART ST

The Coal Exchange

MOUNT STUART SQ

WEST BUTE STREET

JAMES STREET

ADELAIDE ST

STUART STREET

5

ELEANOR PL

WINDSOR ESPLANADE

HAVANNAH STREET

10

DUMBALLS ROAD

HARROWBY ST

A4232

CHANDLERY WAY

CLARENCE BRIDGE

HUNTER ST

BUTE ST

Taff

CORPORATION ROAD

AVONDALE ROAD

CAMBRIDGE STREET

KENT STREET

HOLMESDALE STREET

BROOMFIELD STREET

PENTRE BANK ST

FERRY ROAD

MOORS ROAD

SIGHTS & ATTRACTIONS

Cardiff Bay Visitor Centre
Dubbed 'The Tube', this futuristic visitor centre is an attraction in its own right. The brainchild of William Alsop, the award-winning design built of steel and plywood is in the shape of a giant telescope. Step inside to take in a free exhibition and admire views of the bay. Tourist information and maps are available.
ⓐ Harbour Drive ⓣ 029 2046 3833 ⓦ www.cardiffharbour.com
ⓛ 09.00–18.00 Mon–Sat, 10.30–18.00 Sun (summer); 09.00–18.00 Mon–Sat, 10.30–17.00 Sun (winter)

Cardiff Cats
Soak up Cardiff's sights from the water on a mini-cruise of the bay. Cardiff Cats operates a frequent service to and from the city centre. Hop on at Mermaid Quay, Penarth or the Channel View Leisure Centre.
ⓐ Cardiff Bay ⓣ 07940 142409 ⓦ www.cardiffcats.com ⓛ 11.00–18.00 daily, 18.00–23.00 Saturday night service. Charge

Goleulong 2000 Lightship
This huge red-and-white vessel moored in Cardiff Bay was last stationed off Rhossili on the Gower Peninsula. Effectively a floating church, the vessel now has a peaceful chapel on board. It's free to explore the engine room, cabins and deck.
ⓐ Harbour Drive ⓣ 029 2048 7609 ⓦ www.lightship2000.org.uk
ⓛ 10.00–17.00 Mon–Sat, 14.00–17.00 Sun

▶ *The Goleulong 2000 Lightship in Cardiff Bay*

Norwegian Church

Once a Norwegian seafarer's church in Butetown, this pretty white chapel was moved brick by brick to Cardiff Bay in 1992. Famous children's author Roald Dahl was baptised here in 1916. The intimate venue now houses an art gallery and concert hall staging early music, folk and jazz performances. Rest your feet at the café by the waterfront.
ⓐ Harbour Drive ❶ 029 2045 4899 ❶ 09.00–17.00

Pierhead

The terracotta towers and silver turrets of the Pierhead date back to 1897. The Victorian interior, clocktower and interactive exhibition are highlights of a visit.
ⓐ Maritime Road ❶ 029 2089 8477 ❶ 10.30–18.00 (summer); 09.30–16.30 Mon–Fri, 10.00–16.30 Sat & Sun (winter)

Public Art

Open-air art is high up on the bay's cultural menu. Start at the 70-ft (21-m) Water Tower built entirely of stainless steel, then walk along Mermaid Quay's boardwalk to glimpse the bronze sculpture, *People Like Us*. Next to St David's Hotel & Spa, see the *Drift of Curlews* and the *Rope Knot* sculptures. Near the Pierhead, the *Celtic Ring* marks the sea boundary of the Taff Trail and the striking War Memorial pays homage to the merchant seamen of Cardiff Bay.

Senedd (National Assembly for Wales)

Unveiled by the Queen on St David's Day (1 March) 2006, the National Assembly for Wales dominates the waterfront with its smooth contours and wave-shaped roof. The energy-efficient structure cost a cool £67 million to build and uses the earth for heat and a wind cowl for ventilation. Modern art features include 32 glass panels forming *The Assembly Field* and the fibre-optic *Heart of Wales* set in the chamber's oak floor. Visit the roof to see the debating chamber through the funnel's round windows.

ⓐ Harbour Drive ☎ 029 2089 8261 ⓦ www.wales.gov.uk
🕑 10.30–18.00 Sat & Sun (summer); 08.00–18.00 Mon & Fri, 08.00–20.00 Tues–Thur, 10.30–16.30 Sat & Sun (winter)

Techniquest

Scintillating science is the focus of this hands-on discovery museum. Behind glass walls, kids (and big kids) can test out 160 interactive exhibits from firing a rocket to launching a hot-air balloon, experimenting in the laboratory, or simply studying the stars in the planetarium.

ⓐ Stuart Street ☎ 029 2047 5475 ⓦ www.tquest.org.uk
🕑 09.30–16.30 Mon–Fri, 10.30–17.00 Sat & Sun. Admission charge

The Cardiff Bay Barrage

A marvel of modern engineering, the barrage's 40-m (131-ft) locks and bascule bridges have created a 200-hectare (494-acre) freshwater lake fed by the rivers Taff and Ely. Explore the embankment and get the best views of the waterfront from Barrage Point, shaped like a ship's bow.

ⓐ Cardiff Bay ☎ 029 2087 7900 ⓦ www.cardiffharbour.com
🕑 08.00–20.00 (summer); 08.00–16.00 (winter)

CULTURE

Bay Art Gallery

Pause at this airy gallery to enjoy exhibitions featuring paintings and sculpture by contemporary Welsh and international artists.

ⓐ 54B/C Bute Street ⓣ 029 2065 0016 ⓦ www.bayart.org.uk
ⓛ 11.00–17.00 Tues–Sat, closed Sun & Mon

Butetown History & Art Centre
Focusing on the voice of the people, this pioneering centre traces
local history through photography, art exhibitions, video screenings,
life stories and tours. A visit here is a great way to discover more
about Cardiff Docklands' fascinating past.
ⓐ 5 Dock Chambers, Bute Street ⓣ 029 2025 6757
ⓦ www.bhac.org ⓛ 10.00–17.00 Tues–Fri, 11.00–16.30 Sat & Sun,
closed Mon

CBAT
Explore Welsh, British and international art on canvas at this avant-
garde gallery. The backbone behind a number of public regeneration
schemes, the venue's concept is for art to bring the urban landscape
to life. Exhibitions are free.
ⓐ 123 Bute Street ⓣ 029 2048 8772 ⓦ www.cbat.co.uk ⓛ 10.00–17.00
Tues–Fri, closed Sat–Mon

Millennium Centre
The darling of the bay's performing arts scene, this iconic slate-and-
steel building stages world-class opera, ballet, dance and musicals,
including performances by the resident Welsh National Opera.
The venue hosts free lunchtime and early evening concerts
most days.
ⓐ Bute Place ⓣ Box office: 08700 40 20 00 ⓦ www.wmc.org.uk
ⓛ Open daily

▶ *The Millennium Centre with its stunning fountain*

The Coal Exchange

A commercial hub during Cardiff's coal-exporting heyday, this striking venue has been revamped as one of the city's top art and entertainment centres. The first million-pound deal was struck here in 1907 and the building still stands proud today.
ⓐ Mount Stuart Square ⓣ 029 2049 4917
ⓦ www.coalexchange.co.uk ⓛ Open daily

RETAIL THERAPY

Breze This girlie boutique looks pretty in pink, and stocks a good range of handbags, accessories and ladies' designerwear – including labels like Rene Derhy, Great Plains and Minki Bikini. ⓐ Mermaid Quay ⓛ 10.00–18.00 Mon–Sat, 11.00–17.00 Sun

Craft in the Bay (Makers Guild) This attractive gallery set in a Grade II listed warehouse is the place to find everything from hand-woven wicker to a beautifully embroidered bodice, as well as fine prints, textiles, jewellery and ceramics. ⓐ Lloyd George Avenue ⓣ 029 2048 4611 ⓦ www.makersguildinwales.org.uk ⓛ 10.30–17.30

Mister Natural From camel to cowhide, safari bags to city briefcases, this shop sells a range of high-quality leather bags, suitcases and trunks. You can even pick up a designer dog lead for your pampered pooch. ⓐ West Bute Street ⓣ 029 2049 6813 ⓦ www.misternatural-uk.com ⓛ 10.00–17.30

Riverside Real Food Market Local producers set up stall at this waterfront market. Fill your bags with specialities like hot Welsh cakes, honey and organic lamb, plus fruity chutneys, goats' cheese

and crusty bread. ⓐ Fitzammon Embankment ① 029 2019 0036
ⓦ www.riversidemarket.org.uk ⓛ 10.00–14.00 Sun, closed Mon–Sat

TAKING A BREAK

Bellinis £ ❶ Minimalist chic sums up this smart Italian restaurant
overlooking Mermaid Quay, offering special lunch menus. Try the
sea bass or freshly baked pizza. You can sit on the terrace when the
sun shines. ⓐ Unit 10, Mermaid Quay ① 029 2048 7070
ⓛ 12.00–14.30, 18.00–22.30 Sun–Thur; 12.00–14.30, 18.00–23.00
Fri & Sat

Cadwalader's £ ❷ *Gelati* at their best on the terrace of this ice-
cream parlour in the bay. There's a head-spinning array of dairy
ice creams and smoothies. Choose classic vanilla or be adventurous
with flavours like dragon's breath and chocolate porridge.
ⓐ Mermaid Quay ① 029 2049 7598
ⓦ www.cadwaladersicecream.co.uk
ⓛ 10.00–18.00 Mon–Fri, 10.00–19.00 Sat & Sun

Coffee Mania £ ❸ Whether you're after a frothy coffee, flaky pastry
or a sushi and salad, this sphere-shaped café on the waterfront is a
top choice, offering great views over the bay and value-for-money.
ⓐ Unit 29, Mermaid Quay ① 029 2046 4546 ⓛ 10.30–20.00

Gorge with George £ ❹ It's not just the original name that raises
eyebrows, the no-nonsense menu at this unassuming little place
appeals too. Cheap and cheerful, the calorie-fuelled breakfasts hit
the spot. ⓐ 15 West Bute Street ① 029 2045 6887 ⓛ 07.30–14.00
Mon–Fri, 08.00–11.30 Sat, closed Sun

Harry Ramsden's £ ❺ This popular chain serves proper fish 'n' chips to eat in or take away. ⓐ Stuart Place ⓣ 029 2046 3334 ⓦ www.harryramsdens.co.uk ⓛ 12.00–20.00 Mon–Thur, 12.00–21.00 Fri & Sat, 12.00–19.00 Sun

AFTER DARK

Restaurants

Café Naz £ ❻ Wood floors and white-and-olive colours give this ultra-modern Indian restaurant its unique flair. Feast on contemporary Bangladeshi cuisine and South Indian specialities, and enjoy views of Cardiff Bay. ⓐ 88C Mermaid Quay ⓣ 029 2049 6555 ⓦ www.cafenaz.co.uk ⓛ 12.00–15.00, 18.00–midnight

Signor Valentino's £ ❼ The oak flooring, open-plan kitchen, contemporary art and floor-to-ceiling glass make this modern restaurant a firm favourite among Cardiff's cool crowd. Prices are affordable and the Italian food delicious. ⓐ Unit 15, Mermaid Quay ⓣ 029 2048 2007 ⓦ www.signorvalentino.com ⓛ 12.00–14.30, 18.00–22.30 Mon–Thur; 12.00–15.00, 18.00–23.00 Fri–Sun

Spice Merchant £ ❽ This modern restaurant decked out in bold reds and blues offers authentic Indian fare with a twist. The menu promises spicy food and natural ingredients. It delivers. ⓐ The Big Windsor, Stuart Street ⓣ 029 2049 8984 ⓦ www.spicemerchantcardiff.com ⓛ 11.30–23.30

Scallops ££ ❾ Fish doesn't come much fresher than at this stylish seafood restaurant. From mussels to monkfish, the menu is fairly small but everything is well cooked and presented. Dine alfresco on the terrace with oysters and champagne or a lobster platter. ⓐ Unit 2, Mermaid Quay ⓣ 029 2049 7495 ⓦ www.scallopsrestaurant.com ⓛ 12.00–15.00, 19.00–22.30

Tides Grill £££ ⓾ The 5-star cuisine tempts foodies at St David's Hotel & Spa, with huge glass windows overlooking the bay. Head chef Georg Fuchs cooks with local produce. If your bank balance won't stretch to dinner, enjoy the same views over afternoon tea. ⓐ Havannah Street ⓣ 029 2031 3018 ⓦ www.thestdavidshotel.com ⓛ 12.30–14.15, 15.00–17.00, 18.30–22.30

Bars & clubs
Bute Dock This pub has plenty of local flavour and some great real ales besides. No airs and graces, this is just a good old-fashioned watering hole with darts, occasional live music and a beer garden. ⓐ West Bute Street ⓣ 029 2046 3746 ⓛ 12.00–23.00 Mon–Sat, 12.00–23.30 Sun

Evolution Party people head for this club at The Red Dragon Centre. While one room pumps out dance music, the other entertains with everything from heavy rock to R & B beats. ⓐ Hemingway Road ⓣ 029 2046 4444 ⓦ www.evolution cardiff.co.uk ⓛ 22.00–04.00 Wed, Fri & Sat, closed Sun–Tues & Thur

Salt Young, effortlessly cool and right on the waterfront, this bar-cum-restaurant is always packed. Whether you want to watch live bands or dance till the wee hours, this should be your first stop for a big night out in Cardiff Bay. Cocktails are creative and the atmosphere buzzing. ⓐ Mermaid Quay ⓣ 029 2049 4375 ⓛ 10.00–23.00 Mon–Thur, 10.00–01.00 Fri & Sat, 10.00–22.30 Sun

🔺 *Start your big night out at cool Salt Bar – or Terra Nova across the street*

Terra Nova Shaped like a ship's bow, this glam addition to Cardiff Bay has slender glass windows and stylish balconies. Part of the Brains Brewery clan, the relaxed bar and restaurant span four levels. Few places can beat the views and sparkling Chardonnay on a summer's evening. ⓐ Mermaid Quay ⓣ 029 2045 0947 ⓛ 11.00–midnight Sun–Thur, 11.00–02.00 Fri & Sat

The Eli Jenkins This modern, upmarket pub draws an arty crowd and serves a decent selection of real ales. ⓐ 7–8 Bute Crescent ⓣ 029 2044 0921 ⓛ 12.00–23.30 Mon–Sat, 12.00–22.30 Sun

The Glee Club Cardiff's top comedy club is the place to come to giggle and guffaw. One compere, three live acts and beer on tap keep punters amused. This venue has the cream of the comedy crop, followed by a disco at weekends. ⓐ Mermaid Quay ⓣ 0870 241 5093 ⓦ www.glee.co.uk ⓛ Thur–Sat, closed Sun–Wed; check times for individual shows

The Point Live music draws night owls to this huge venue in a converted church, with a high-tech sound system. Featuring a mix of up-and-coming and established bands, plus funky club nights, you can party surrounded by stained-glass windows, vaulted ceilings and gothic arches. ⓐ Mount Stuart Square ⓣ 029 2046 0873 ⓦ www.thepointcardiffbay.com

The Waterguard A castle? A stately home? Nope. As the sign outside states: 'It's a pub. And it's open.' Thirsty punters looking for quality beers, a laid-back atmosphere and somewhere quiet enough to have a good chat are in the right place. The service is friendly and bar snacks keep hunger at bay. ⓐ Harbour Drive ⓣ 029 2049 9034 ⓛ 12.00–23.00 Mon–Sat, 12.00–22.30 Sun

The Wharf An impressive red-brick building houses this sprawling bar and restaurant. Thursday night welcomes first-class comedy to the stage. The vibe is relaxed and the crowd out for a good time. ⓐ 121 Schooner Way ⓣ 029 2040 5092 ⓛ 11.00–midnight Mon–Thur, 11.00–01.00 Fri & Sat, 11.00–23.00 Sun

Cathays

Cathays is pinned at the capital's civic heart. While most visitors make a beeline for the vast National Museum & Gallery, it's worth lingering to see what else this corner of Cardiff has to offer. And that's plenty. The wealth that coal brought during the 19th century is reflected in the manicured gardens and fine Edwardian buildings, avant-garde theatres and captivating art galleries.

❶ Pick up a map of the Cardiff Centenary Walk from the tourist office to take in the main sights.

SIGHTS & ATTRACTIONS

Alexandra Gardens

This pocket of greenery is a pleasant spot to relax beside the flowers and cedar trees, and watch the world go by. The garden is at its best in spring, when it's awash with tulips and pink cherry trees.
ⓐ Cathays Park ⓛ Open daily

Cardiff University

You can't fail to miss this white-stone, neoclassical building in the civic centre. Built at the turn of the century, this imposing structure is the university's main building. If you want to enter the campus, get permission from the porters first.
ⓐ Park Place

Cathays Cemetery

One of Britain's largest Victorian cemeteries, this peaceful and atmospheric site spans several hundred acres. The 3-km (2-mile)

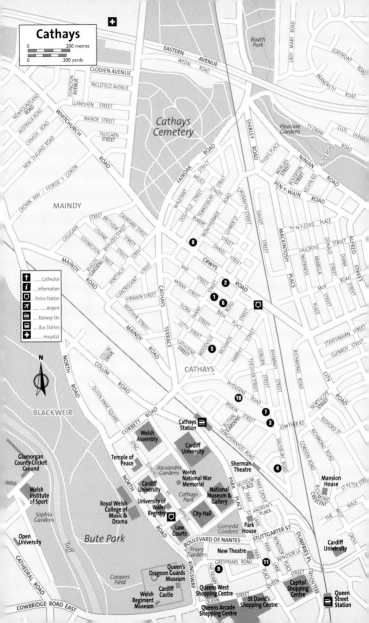

Heritage Trail traces the cemetery's history, taking a glimpse
at Cardiff's famous past residents and memorials featuring
Victorian symbolism.

ⓐ Fairoak Road ⓛ Open daily

City Hall

A Welsh dragon perches on the domed roof of this Renaissance-style
building, carved from white Portland stone. A sweeping staircase
leads to the Marble Hall, housing 11 marble statues of Welsh heroes
including St David. The extensive art collection, oak-panelled Council
Chamber and ornate Assembly Rooms are also worth a visit.

ⓐ Cathays Park ⓣ 029 2087 1727 ⓛ 09.00–18.00 Mon–Sat,
closed Sun

Friary Gardens

These small but perfectly formed gardens are framed with neat
hedges and clipped bushes, planted in honour of the third Marquess
of Bute. A break here provides respite from the city's buzz.

ⓐ Cathays Park ⓛ Open daily

Gorsedd Gardens

Stroll shady paths in these gardens, one of Cardiff's best-kept secrets.
Spy the bronze statues of Lord Ninian Stuart and John Cory rising
from the bushes, and the famous Gorsedd Circle – a ceremonial set
of stones that have been a feature of the park since 1899.

ⓐ Cathays Park ⓛ Open daily

Law Courts

Standing in leafy Cathays Park and flanking the City Hall, the city's
grand Law Courts date back to 1904. Glimpse the obelisk-style

lamps bearing Cardiff's coat of arms and the statue of Judge
Gwilym Williams.

ⓐ Cathays Park

Park House

This gothic-style gem completed in 1875 is the brainchild
of acclaimed architect William Burges. Today, the grey
sandstone building is one of Cardiff's most iconic
19th-century townhouses.

ⓐ Park Place

Temple of Peace

A gift from Lord David Davies of Llandinam to the Welsh people, this
classical T-shaped building pays homage to those who lost their
lives in World War I. The red-roofed structure shelters the marble
Temple Hall, wood-panelled Council Chamber and the Crypt
housing the first Welsh Book of Remembrance.

ⓐ Cathays Park

University of Wales Registry

Spot Cathays Park's first building, characterised by its Ionic columns,
round windows and ever-photogenic sleeping dragons adorning the
front posts.

ⓐ King Edward VII Avenue

Welsh National War Memorial

At Alexandra Gardens' centre, you'll find this sunken court with
Corinthian columns and bronze figures to commemorate the men
that lost their lives in World War I.

ⓐ Alexandra Gardens

CULTURE

National Museum & Gallery

Moving from art gems to archaeology, natural history to geology, this superb museum is a cultural highlight of any visit to Cardiff, showcasing one of Europe's best Impressionist collections. It's the place to come if you want to admire Monet and van Gogh, Celtic coins and cannon balls all under one roof. Highlights stretch from Picasso prints to contemporary Welsh stoneware. Kids love the Evolution of Wales, tracing the country's history back millions of years to the age of dinosaurs.

ⓐ Cathays Park ☎ 029 2039 7951 🖶 029 2057 3321
🌐 www.nmgw.ac.uk ⏰ 10.00–17.00 Tues–Sun, closed Mon

New Theatre

Entertainment is synonymous with this Edwardian venue, whether your idea of a good night out is a glitzy West End show, modern ballet or poignant drama. Diversions (The Dance Company of Wales) perform powerful choreographies during their home season here, welcoming some of Europe's top dancers to the stage.

ⓐ Park Place ☎ 029 2087 8889 🌐 www.newtheatrecardiff.co.uk
⏰ Open daily

Sherman Theatre

Youth theatre is the essence of this energetic performing arts venue. The programme is a fusion of experimental productions, drama adaptations and family musicals. One of the major cultural

◀ *The National Museum & Gallery has a fantastic Impressionist collection*

venues in South Wales, the theatre has a resident company that cultivates new talent.

🅐 Senghennydd Road 🕿 029 2064 6900
🅦 www.shermantheatre.co.uk 🕒 Open daily

TAKING A BREAK

Café Junior £ ❶ Families flock to this child-friendly, light-filled café, where adults can sip cappuccino on comfy sofas while the little ones play. The health-conscious menu is mostly organic; try the potato waffles, paninis and fresh fruit smoothies. 🅐 Fanny Street 🕿 029 2034 5653 🅦 http://cafejunior.com 🕒 09.30–18.00

Café Mina £ ❷ For a delicious Lebanese lunch, this relaxed restaurant beckons. Munch on mezze, stuffed vine leaves and spicy meatballs, plus Middle Eastern snacks like vegetarian falafels.
🅐 43 Crwys Road 🕿 029 2023 5212 🅦 www.cafemina.co.uk
🕒 12.00–14.30 Fri–Sun, 17.00–23.30 Mon–Sun

Daiquiris £ ❸ With a name like this you'd be forgiven for thinking cocktails, but what you'll actually get is a freshly made baguette.
🅐 49 Salisbury Road 🕿 029 2034 4807 🕒 10.00–22.00

Dough £ ❹ Refuel with a bagel and latte at this cheap and cheerful student haunt. 🅐 20 Salisbury Road 🕿 029 2022 2888
🕒 08.00–17.00

Greenhouse Café £ ❺ A real find for vegetarians, this cosy café often has a choice of just three dishes, but each is cooked to perfection. It's a nice spot to have lunch with the locals.

⊚ 38 Woodville Road ☏ 029 2023 5731 ⏱ 12.00–14.00, 17.30–23.30 Mon–Sat, closed Sun

AFTER DARK

Restaurants
Aegean Taverna £ ❻ Great if you're dining in a group, this lively restaurant serves tasty Greek food with copious amounts of retsina. Sample specialities like stuffed calamari and meze, rounded off with sticky baklavas and perhaps some Greek dancing to the bouzouki … ⊚ 117 Woodville Road ☏ 029 2034 5114 ⓦ www.aegeantaverna.co.uk ⏱ 18.30–23.00 Mon–Sat, closed Sun

Fortune House £ ❼ As the name clearly points out, you are indeed pretty lucky to eat here. Expect generous portions, great Chinese food and friendly staff. The all-you-can-eat emperor's choice menu comes recommended. All dishes are cooked to order and your plate just keeps refilling. ⊚ 43–45 Salisbury Road ☏ 029 2064 1311 ⏱ 12.00–14.00, 17.30–23.30 Mon–Sat, closed Sun

Phi-b's £ ❽ Enjoy authentic Chinese with a modern twist at this sleek venue, a favourite among those craving a little spice. The prices won't blow the budget either. ⊚ 98 Crwys Road ☏ 029 2039 8352 ⏱ 12.00–14.00, 17.30–23.30 Sun–Thur, 12.00–14.00, 17.00–midnight Fri & Sat

The Grill £ ❾ This sleek diner exudes New York cool. It's a fun place to come with friends before popping into Tiger Tiger (see page 102). The all-American menu features steaks from the grill and salads. Sink your teeth into a signature gourmet burger. ⊚ The Friary ☏ 029 2039 1944 ⓦ www.thegrillat.co.uk ⏱ 17.00–midnight

Armless Dragon ££ ⑩   The freshest local produce lands on your plate at this hidden gem. Well-presented dishes include tender Brecon lamb, flavoursome black beef and laverballs. The secret to this contemporary Welsh cooking is in the fine ingredients. You'll find the menu chalked up on a blackboard. ⓐ 97 Wyeverne Road ⓣ 029 2038 2357 ⓛ 12.00–14.30 Tues–Fri, 19.00–21.30 Tues–Sat, closed Sun & Mon

Da Venditto ££ ⑪   Imaginative Italian flavours tempt at this award-winning restaurant in a trendy basement opposite the New Theatre. The décor is smart, the wine list extensive and the service efficient. ⓐ 7–8 Park Place ⓣ 029 2023 0781 ⓦ www.vendittogroup. co.uk ⓛ 12.00–14.30, 18.00–22.30 Tues–Sat, closed Sun & Mon

Bars & clubs

Cantaloop   Posh with a capital P, this upmarket bar in a listed building is opposite the New Theatre. The style is contemporary chic, with polished wood floors and chocolate-brown chairs. Try a vodka-fuelled Bay Breeze cocktail and tapas in the intimate lounge. ⓐ Greyfriars Road ⓣ 029 2023 3833 ⓦ www.cantaloopbar.com ⓛ 11.00–03.00 Fri & Sat, closed Sun–Thur

Creation   This club keeps partygoers on their toes from dusk till dawn. A firm favourite among blurry-eyed students, the late-night venue spins a mix of old skool, dance anthems and R & B. ⓐ Greyfriars Road ⓣ 029 2037 7014 ⓦ www.creationcardiff.com ⓛ 22.00–03.00 Mon, 22.00–05.00 Fri, 22.00–03.00 Sat, closed Sun, Tues–Thur

---

▶ *Stop for a moment at the National War Memorial in Alexandra Gardens*

Cuba Fancy some *merengue* with your mojito? Latino grooves and dirty-dancing moves make this popular student bar rock by night. The cocktails and bar snacks are fairly priced, and the party vibe invites strutting on the dance floor. ⓐ The Friary ☎ 029 2039 7967 🕒 11.30–midnight Mon, Wed & Thur, 11.30–02.00 Tues, Fri & Sat, closed Sun

Ha Ha's It's not just the name that raises smiles. This big, cheery bar is a popular option, serving live music and cheap drinks. ⓐ The Friary Centre ☎ 029 2039 7997 🕒 11.00–23.00 Mon–Sat, 10.00–22.30 Sun

Henry's Bar Smarter than some of its neighbours, this pre-theatre venue has a pleasant terrace and an open-plan bar serving a decent selection of wines, cocktails and beers. ⓐ 8–16 Park Place ☎ 029 2022 4672 🕒 11.00–23.00 Mon–Sat, 12.00–22.30 Sun

Incognito A favourite student haunt, this modern venue has a relaxed feel and funky music. Come early to make the most of the happy hour, or at the weekend when the place teems with young, beautiful people. ⓐ 29 Park Place ☎ 029 2041 2190 🕒 11.00–23.00 Mon & Tues, 11.00–02.00 Wed–Sat, 12.00–00.30 Sun

Park Vaults Expect a relaxed atmosphere at this snug pub in the Thistle Hotel, which has kept its Victorian charm. Perfect for a quiet drink or chat with friends, come here to enjoy real ale, relax or watch the game. ⓐ Park Place ☎ 029 2038 3471 🕒 11.00–23.00 Mon–Sat, closed Sun

▶ *Take in a show at the New Theatre (see page 95)*

Pen & Wig The Cathays classic, this oak-panelled pub exudes charm. Snuggle up in a leather armchair by the fire or cool down with a pint in the walled beer garden. @ 1 Park Grove ☎ 029 2064 9091 🕐 10.00–midnight Mon–Fri, 10.00–01.00 Sat & Sun

Slug & Lettuce Wood floors and leather sofas set the scene in this central chain, with a good range of draught and bottled beers. @ The Friary Centre ☎ 029 2022 5063 🖥 www.slugandlettuce.co.uk 🕐 11.00–23.00 Mon–Fri, 10.00–23.00 Sat, 10.00–22.30 Sun

The End Put on your 'beer goggles' for cheap pints at this lively student pub. The vibe is laid-back, with squishy sofas, table football and a pool table. The End? No. The night has only just begun … @ Coburn Street ☎ 029 2037 3897 🕐 11.00–23.00 Mon–Sat, 12.00–22.30 Sun

The Flora No fuss, no frills, just a traditional, friendly pub that's popular with the locals who come here to watch rugby on the big screen or chill in the beer garden. It's also a WiFi hotspot. @ 136 Cathays Terrace ☎ 029 2040 5039 🕐 11.00–23.00 Mon–Sat, 12.00–22.30 Sun

Tiger Tiger A night out at this ultra-chic bar and club is a treat for the senses – from mosaics and wood screens in the Medina to minimalist chic in the Tiger Bar and mirrored columns in the club upstairs. Sip creative cocktails, snack on tasty bar food and mingle with Cardiff's cool crowd. @ The Friary ☎ 029 2039 1944 🖥 www.tigertiger-cardiff.co.uk 🕐 12.00–02.00 Mon–Sat, 12.00–00.30 Sun

---

▶ *The wide expanse of Dunraven Bay (see page 107)*

OUT OF TOWN
trips

Glamorgan Heritage Coast

Stretching from Aberthaw to Porthcawl, the 23-km (14-mile) Glamorgan Heritage Coast beckons with secluded coves, clear waters and craggy cliffs. Whether you want to walk golden dunes, grab a wetsuit to hit the surf, or climb Celtic castles, this compact coastline in South Wales is wild and wonderful. Two legs or two wheels and you're off!

GETTING THERE

The Glamorgan Heritage Coast is easy to access by public transport. Penarth is just a 20-minute bus ride from central Cardiff (Bus 92), and Arriva Trains (❶ 08457 48 49 50 ⓦ www.arrivatrainswales.co.uk) operates a good service from Cardiff Central Station to Barry Island, Penarth and Bridgend via Llantwit Major. Other useful routes include the X2 from Cardiff to Porthcawl via Bridgend and the X91 from Cardiff to Llantwit Major. If you're driving, look out for junctions 33 to 37 on the M4 motorway.

SIGHTS & ATTRACTIONS

Bryngarw Country Park

The mighty oaks and mossy wetlands of this 46-hectare (113-acre) reserve lie just north of Bridgend. Colour-coded trails weave through countryside dotted with lakes and rivers. Relax by the magnolias and maples in the oriental garden, or spot buzzards and woodpeckers.

ⓐ Brynmenyn, near Bridgend ❶ 01656 725155 ⓛ Open daily

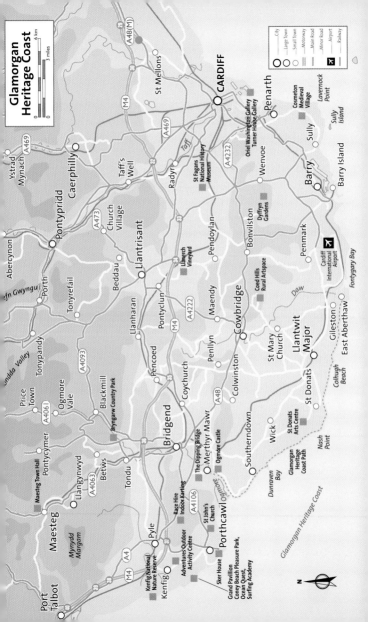

Glamorgan Heritage Coast

Legend:
- City
- Large Town
- Small Town
- Main Road
- Motorway
- Minor Road
- Railway

0 3 miles
0 6 km

CARDIFF

Penarth
Cosmeton Medieval Village
Lavernock Point
Sully
Sully Island
Barry
Barry Island

St Mellons
Oriel Washington Gallery
Turner House Gallery

Caerphilly
Taff's Well
Radyr
St Fagans National History Museum
Wenvoe

Ystrad Mynach
Pontypridd
Church Village
Llanharan
Llantrisant
Beddau
Tonyrefail
Llanerch Vineyard
Pendoylan
Maendy
Dyffryn Gardens
Bonvilston
Penmark
Cardiff International Airport
Fontygary Bay

Abercynon
Cefn Gwyngu
Porth
Tonypandy
Rhondda Valley

Price Town
Ogmore Vale
Blackmill
Bryngarw Country Park
Pencoed
Coychurch
Penllyn
Cowbridge
Coed Hills Rural Artspace

St Mary Church
Colwinston
Llantwit Major
Gileston
East Aberthaw

Maesteg
Maesteg Town Hall
Pontycymer
Llangynwyd
Betws
Tondu
Bridgend
Merthyr Mawr
Ogmore Castle
The Dipping Bridge
Southerndown
Wick
St Donats Arts Centre
St Donats
Colhugh Beach

Mynydd Margam
Pyle
Race Hire Indoor Karting
St John's Church
Porthcawl
Ogmore
Glamorgan Heritage Coast Path
Dunraven Bay
Nash Point

Port Talbot
Kenfig
Kenfig National Nature Reserve
Adventures Outdoor Activity Centre
Sker House
Grand Pavilion
Coney Beach Pleasure Park,
Ocean Quest,
Surfing Academy

Glamorgan Heritage Coast

N

Dyffryn Gardens

Cardiff and surrounding districts have got a few surprises up their green sleeves, and this Grade I listed Edwardian garden is one of them. Bury your head in fragrant rhododendrons and roses, stroll the vine walk, or take in the Victorian ferns and lavender court in the 22-hectare (55-acre) grounds.

🄰 St Nicholas 🕓 029 2059 1966 🄦 www.dyffryngardens.org.uk
🕔 10.00–18.00 (summer); 10.00–17.00 (winter). Admission charge

Kenfig National Nature Reserve

This reserve shelters a huge dune system that once spanned Wales' entire south coast. Enjoy sweeping coastal views or explore the area on an 11-km (7-mile) circular walk via Kenfig Castle and Sker House. The excellent visitor centre offers more information.

🄰 Ton Kenfig, Pyle 🕓 01656 743386 🕔 14.00–16.30 Mon–Fri, 10.00–16.30 Sat & Sun

Merthyr Mawr

Thatched cottages cluster around the green of this idyllic village. Surrounded by woodlands and meadows, it's the perfect spot for a lazy picnic. Glimpse the eerie remains of Candleston Castle, all that is left of an estate that vanished beneath the sands.

🕓 CADW (Welsh Historic Monuments Executive Agency): 01443 336000

Ogmore Castle

Explore the remains of this enchanting Norman stone-built castle beside the River Ewenny. Skip over the 52 stepping stones crossing the river to Merthyr Mawr, but check tide times first so you don't get stranded.

🄰 Ogmore 🕓 CADW: 01443 336000

Sker House

Spooky Sker House is one of Wales' most haunted buildings, recently rescued from dereliction. The Maid of Sker was once imprisoned in the Grade I listed manor and apparently her ghost can now be seen at the window. The house is not currently open to the public.

🅐 Near Porthcawl

Southerndown (Dunraven Bay)

Smooth sands and lofty limestone cliffs make this one of the Heritage Coast's most scenic spots. To the east is Witches' Point and to the west the Ogmore Deeps. Before setting off in search of fossils, check the tides at the visitor centre.

🅘 Glamorgan Heritage Coast Centre: 01656 880157

🔺 *Mountaineering sheep at Ogmore Castle*

St John's Church

Originally a fortress, Newton's limestone church dates back to the
12th century. The hidden gem here is St John's Well. In the Middle
Ages, superstitious locals believed the well possessed magical
properties, as it was mysteriously full when the tide was low and
empty when it was high.

ⓐ Newton ⓛ Open daily

The Dipping Bridge

Spy the holes in the parapets at this 15th-century bridge, where
shepherds once pushed their sheep into the River Ogmore to give
them a 'dip'. The bridge also has a sinister side: the New Inn that
once stood here was home to a landlord that murdered pilgrims
en route to St David's shrine.

ⓐ Merthyr Mawr ⓘ CADW: 01443 336000

CULTURE

Coed Hills Rural Artspace

Art meets the environment at this eco-friendly gallery. Walk the
woodland sculpture trail or learn more about straw bale building
and solar water heating.

ⓐ St Hilary, Cowbridge ⓣ 01446 774084
ⓦ www.coedhills.co.uk ⓛ 10.00 till dusk

Grand Pavilion

The domed theatre on Porthcawl's seafront stages a variety of
festivals, comedy, musical theatre and children's shows.

ⓐ The Esplanade, Porthcawl ⓣ 01656 786996
ⓦ www.grandpavilion.co.uk

Maesteg Town Hall

Maesteg's striking grey-and-red stone town hall houses a theatre presenting concerts and drama, plus exhibitions including paintings by Welsh artist Christopher Williams.

ⓐ Talbot Street, Maesteg ⓣ 01656 733269
ⓦ www.maestegtownhall.co.uk

Oriel Washington Gallery

Fresh-faced and original, this gallery showcases contemporary Welsh art by the sea. It's also a good place to pick up local crafts such as pottery and handmade jewellery.

ⓐ Stanwell Road, Penarth ⓣ 029 2071 2100
ⓦ www.washingtongallery.co.uk ⓒ 09.30–17.30 Mon–Sat,
11.00–17.00 Sun

🔺 *Taking a dip at The Dipping Bridge*

St Donats Arts Centre
A medieval barn converted into a state-of-the-art theatre, this venue lures culture vultures with everything from live jazz and classical concerts to art-house cinema and comedy.
ⓐ St Donats ⓣ 01446 799100 ⓦ www.stdonats.com

Turner House Gallery
It's free to admire fine arts at this little gem of a gallery in Penarth, an extension of Cardiff's National Museum & Gallery.
ⓐ Plymouth Road, Penarth ⓣ 029 2070 8870 ⓛ 10.00–17.00 Tues–Fri, closed Sat–Mon

RECREATION

Adventures Outdoor Activity Centre
Gorge scrambling or quad biking? This is the place for the ultimate adrenaline rush, with activities from rock climbing and mountain biking to canoeing and hiking. ⓐ Kenfig, Porthcawl ⓣ 01656 782300 ⓦ www.adventureswales.co.uk ⓛ 16.00–20.00 Mon–Fri (advance booking only), 10.00–17.00 Sat & Sun

Coney Beach Pleasure Park
Twist and turn to your heart's content on Porthcawl's seafront. Thrill-seekers should make a beeline for the Megablitz rollercoaster. ⓐ Eastern Promenade, Porthcawl ⓣ 01656 788911 ⓛ 15.00–22.00 (times depend on weather, check in advance)

Cosmeton Medieval Village
Stepping back in time to the Middle Ages, this reconstructed 14th-century village offers tours with costumed villagers. ⓐ Country Park,

Penarth ❶ 029 2070 1678 🕐 11.00–17.00 (summer); 11.00–16.00 (winter). Admission charge

Glamorgan Heritage Coast Path

Explore the hidden nooks of the 23-km (14-mile) Heritage Coast on foot. A trail hugs the length of the coast, from East Aberthaw to Merthyr Mawr's dunes. En route you'll see jagged rocks and sandy bays, Norman castles and Celtic hill settlements. Keep to the cliff paths and watch out for changing tides.

Llanerch Vineyard

Taste the grape at Wales' largest vineyard, producing award-winning Cariad wines. Round off your self-guided tour of the vineyard with a tasting of elderflowery whites and fruity rosés. ⓐ Hensol, Pendoylan ❶ 01443 225877 ⓦ www.llanerch-vineyard.co.uk 🕐 10.00–17.00. Admission charge

Ocean Quest

Making the most of Porthcawl's waves, this centre is a top choice for scuba diving, surfing, wakeboarding and kayaking. Take a course with trained professionals or hire equipment and hit the water. ⓐ Porthcawl ❶ 01656 783310 ⓦ www.ocean-quest.co.uk

Race Hire Indoor Karting

Life is in the fast lane at this indoor karting track at Stormy Down Airfield. Apparently the sensation is the closest you'll get to Formula One racing. ⓐ Stormy Down, near Bridgend ❶ 01656 773737 🕐 10.00–17.30 Mon–Sat, closed Sun

Surfing Academy
Follow the 'Learn to Surf' sign to let off some excess energy balancing on a board. Simon Tucker teaches the surfing A–Z at Rest Bay, awarded the Blue Flag for its clean waters. ⓐ Rest Bay, Porthcawl ⓣ 01656 772415 ⓦ www.surfingexperience.com

RETAIL THERAPY

Ewenny Pottery It's a pleasure to potter around this craft centre, where Alun Jenkins is a whiz on the wheel. The workshop stocks quality glazed earthenware made from local red clay. ⓐ Ewenny ⓣ 01656 653020 ⓦ www.ewennypottery.com ⓒ 09.30–17.00 Mon–Sat, closed Sun

Makers Gallery A unique collection of crafts including pottery, embroidery, glassware and paintings tempt you to loosen your purse strings at this high-street gallery. ⓐ 74 Eastgate, Cowbridge ⓣ 01446 775280 ⓒ 10.00–13.00, 14.00–17.00 Mon, Tues, Thur–Sat, closed Wed & Sun

McArthurGlen Designer Outlet Village Bag a bargain on designer labels at this outlet village, where 100 shops offer up to a 50 per cent discount on top brands from Karen Millen to Calvin Klein. There's also a food court, nine-screen cinema and play area. ⓐ The Derwen, Bridgend ⓣ 01656 665700 ⓦ www.bridgenddesigneroutlet.com ⓒ 10.00–20.00 Mon–Fri, 10.00–19.00 Sat, 10.00–17.00 Sun

Old Wool Barn Art and Craft Centre Browse the work of local artists and designers at this studio workshop set in a pretty courtyard.

🅐 Verity's Court, Cowbridge 🕿 01446 773012 🕒 10.00–16.00

Red Dot Gallery Funky jewellery, contemporary crafts and original prints share shelf space at this bright, modern gallery. 🅐 The Limes, Cowbridge 🕿 01446 771715 🕒 10.00–17.00 Tues–Sat, closed Sun & Mon

Rhiw Shopping Centre Wall-to-wall high-street shops cluster under one roof at this Bridgend mall. The indoor market is the place to sniff out local produce. 🅐 Bridgend 🕿 01656 658704 🅦 www.rhiwshopping.com 🕒 08.00–18.00 Mon–Sat, 10.00–16.00 Sun

TAKING A BREAK

Angel Inn £ Conveniently located for Kenfig National Nature Reserve, this cosy 13th-century village pub serves generous lunches. Hearty specials include home-made steak and ale pie. The food is good and prices very reasonable. 🅐 Marlas Road, Mawdlam, near Pyle 🕿 01656 740456 🕒 11.00–23.00 Mon–Sat, 12.00–22.30 Sun

Plough and Harrow £ A pit stop on the 8-km (5-mile) circular Nash Point to Monknash walk, this traditional pub is a top choice for lunch and a pint of real ale. 🅐 Monknash, near Llantwit Major 🕿 01656 890209 🕒 Serves food 12.00–14.30, 18.00–21.00 Mon–Sat, 12.00–14.30 Sun

Sidoli's £ Rest your feet in Porthcawl at this friendly place serving tasty snacks and a good old-fashioned cup of tea. 🅐 18 John Street, Porthcawl 🕿 01656 783539 🕒 08.00–17.00

Tempus Fugit £ Garlicky prawns, stuffed peppers and thick slices of tortilla are staples on the menu at this tapas bar, next to Ogmore post office. Sit on the terrace to glimpse Hardy's Bay. ⓐ 87 Main Road, Ogmore-by-Sea ⓣ 01656 880661 ⓦ www.tempusfugitogmore.co.uk ⓛ 10.00–14.00, 18.00–21.00

AFTER DARK

Blue Anchor Inn £ A favourite among locals, this atmospheric pub with its thatched roof and stone walls dates back to 1380. Pull up a chair by the fire to drink a pint of Brains Bitter, refuel with tasty bar snacks or book a table in the restaurant. ⓐ East Aberthaw, near Barry ⓣ 01446 750329 ⓦ www.blueanchoraberthaw.com ⓛ 12.00–14.00, 19.00–21.00 Mon–Sat, 12.30–14.30 Sun

Frolics Restaurant £ The imaginative French menu at this Southerndown restaurant features fresh, unfussy dishes like smoked haddock risotto, plus a decent choice of wines. The clifftop location gives great views over the Bristol Channel. ⓐ Beach Road, Southerndown ⓣ 01656 880127 ⓛ 12.00–14.30, 18.30–22.00 Tues–Sat, 12.00–14.30 Sun, closed Mon

Mediterraneo £ A converted boathouse on Penarth seafront, this inviting Italian restaurant hits the spot with an alfresco aperitif on the terrace, followed by well-cooked seafood, pasta or risotto. ⓐ 10 The Esplanade, Penarth ⓣ 029 2070 3428 ⓦ www.mediterraneopenarth.com ⓛ 12.00–23.00

The Bear Hotel £–££ This 12th-century hotel and restaurant in Cowbridge serves a slice of history with its home-cooked food and real ales. Enjoy a drink by the fire in the lounge, or venture to the stone-vaulted cellar for à la carte cuisine after dark. ⓐ 63 High Street, Cowbridge ⓣ 01446 774814 ⓦ www.bearhotel.com ⓛ 19.00–21.30

The Olive Tree ££ Expect fresh Welsh fare with a French twist and efficient service at this little restaurant in Penarth. Savour specialities like Glamorgan sausages served with a Roquefort cream sauce. ⓐ 21 Glebe Street, Penarth ⓣ 029 2070 7077 ⓦ www.the-olive-tree.net ⓛ 18.00–21.00 Tues–Fri, 19.00–21.30 Sat, 12.00–14.30 Sun

△ *The seafront and Grand Pavilion at Porthcawl*

ACCOMMODATION

Acorn Camping and Caravan Site £ Camp on the coast at this tranquil site in Llantwit Major, set in open farmland near the beach. The facilities include free hot showers, a shop, playground, laundry and games room. ⓐ Rose Dew Farm, Llantwit Major ① 01446 794024 ⓦ www.campingandcaravansites.co.uk

Blue Seas B&B £ Right on the water's edge, this family-run B&B overlooking Newton's beach is a sound choice. Modern single and twin rooms have washbasin and tea-making facilities. ⓐ 72 Beach Road, Newton ① 01656 786540 ⓦ www.blueseasbnb.co.uk

Bryngarw House £ Set in a country park near Bridgend, this manor house combines 18th-century charm with modern creature comforts in the 19 en-suite rooms. Dine at The Harlequin restaurant, or walk one of the trails leading to valleys and hilltops. ⓐ Bryngarw Country Park, Brynmenyn, near Bridgend ① 01656 729009

Crossways Manor House ££ Surrounded by 2 hectares (6 acres) of grounds, this greystone mansion has bags of character and is surprisingly affordable. Details like the central cupola, winding oak staircase and brass chandeliers add to the charm. Elegant rooms are bright and spacious, and the Welsh breakfast substantial. ⓐ Cowbridge ① 01446 773171 ⓦ www.crosswayshouse.co.uk

Edmon Guest House ££ This smart, well-kept town house in Porthcawl is just a few steps from the beach. En-suite rooms are clean, bright and comfortable. Family rooms also available. ⓐ 33 Esplanade Avenue, Porthcawl ① 01656 788102 ⓦ www.edmonguesthouse.co.uk

Llanerch Vineyard ££ Go back to nature at this romantic B&B in the Vale of Glamorgan. Surrounded by vines and forest, enjoy wine tastings and long walks in the woods. Its offbeat location means you'll need your own set of wheels. ⓐ Hensol, Pendoylan ⓣ 01443 225877 ⓦ www.llanerch-vineyard.co.uk

Plas Llanmihangel ££ Tucked away in a green and secluded spot, this 13th-century Grade I listed manor is a real find. Explore the baronial hall and centuries-old tower, or stroll to the nearby ruins of Beaupre Castle. ⓐ Llanmihangel, near Cowbridge ⓣ 01446 774610

Protea House ££ An Edwardian townhouse just a minute's walk from Porthcawl's seafront, the rooms here have crisp white linen, pine furniture and plenty of natural light. ⓐ 25 Esplanade Avenue, Porthcawl ⓣ 01656 786526

The Old Barn B&B ££ Nature-lovers find respite at this beautifully converted 17th-century barn. Oozing country charm, the guesthouse has a peaceful garden overlooking the Vale of Glamorgan. Comfortable rooms with oak beams and slate floors have all mod cons. ⓐ The Croft, Penmark ⓣ 01446 711352 ⓦ www.theoldbarnbedandbreakfast.co.uk

White House ££ Near the beach and 5 minutes' walk from Llantwit Major village, this Georgian house has a friendly feel. The all-important touches are there – from spacious bedrooms to fluffy bathrobes and luxury toiletries. ⓐ Flanders Road, Llantwit Major ⓣ 01446 794250 ⓦ www.waleswhitehouse.co.uk

The Gower Peninsula & Swansea Bay

The first place in Britain to be designated an area of outstanding natural beauty, the Gower Peninsula has earned its title. An hour's drive to the west of Cardiff, this 31-km (19-mile) stretch of unspoilt coast, moors and heathland is where the Bristol Channel meets the wild Atlantic. And it's the sea that has shaped the sheltered coves and sandy beaches studding the coastline. From Palaeolithic caves to romantic ruins, Iron Age forts to prehistoric standing stones, the peninsula is a heady mix of coast and culture.

GETTING THERE

An hour's train or bus ride from Cardiff Central station takes you to Swansea, the gateway to the Gower Peninsula. If you're driving, take the M4 and exit at junction 42 for Swansea Bay, or junction 47 for north Gower. The 'Walking by Bus' initiative makes getting around Gower easy for those without a car. Buses from Swansea shuttle visitors to four walking routes. Swansea tourist information centre offers more details (☎ 01792 468321 ⓦ www.visitswanseabay.com).

SIGHTS & ATTRACTIONS

Arthur's Stone
This monster of a rock has an impressive history to match its size. A neolithic burial chamber dubbed Arthur's Stone, the 25-tonne, 4-m (13-ft) high boulder dates back to 2500 BC.

Steeped in legend, the mysterious megalith has been associated with King Arthur and St David.
ⓐ Cefn Bryn

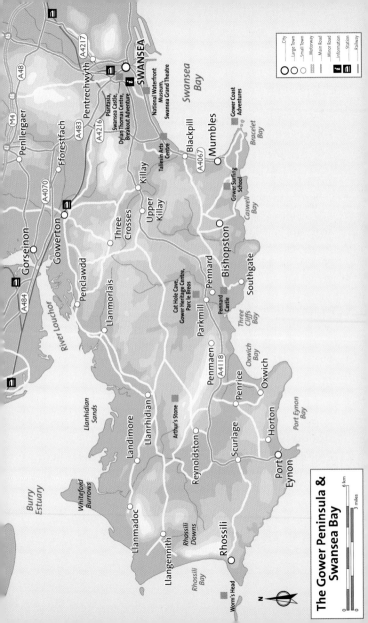

The Gower Peninsula & Swansea Bay

SWANSEA

Plantasia,
Swansea Castle,
Dylan Thomas Centre,
Breakout Adventure

National Waterfront Museum
Swansea Grand Theatre

Swansea Bay

Gower Coast Adventures

Bracelet Bay

Mumbles

Blackpill

A4067

Taliesin Arts Centre

Gower Surfing School

Caswell Bay

Killay

Upper Killay

Bishopston

Three Crosses

Southgate

Pennard

Penclawdd

Cat Hole Cave,
Gower Heritage Centre,
Parc le Breos

Pennard Castle

Three Cliffs Bay

Llanmorlais

Parkmill

Penmaen

Oxwich Bay

A4118

Oxwich

Llanrhidian

Arthur's Stone

Penrice

Port Eynon Bay

Landimore

Reynoldston

Scurlage

Horton

Llanhidian Sands

Port Eynon

Burry Estuary

Whiteford Burrows

Llanmadoc

Llangennith

Rhossili Downs

Rhossili

Rhossili Bay

Worm's Head

N

Gorseinon

Penllergaer

Fforestfach

Gowerton

Pentrechwyth

A48
M4
A4217
A483
A4216
A4070
A484

River Loughor

Key
City
Large Town
Small Town
Motorway
Main Road
Minor Road
Information
Station
Railway

6 km
3 miles

Bracelet Bay

Clean waters wash over the smooth limestone pebbles on this pretty bay, awarded a Blue Flag for cleanliness. Explore the rock pools, spot the white lighthouse guarding the headland or take a 10-minute stroll to Mumbles.

Cat Hole Cave

Follow the footpath from the Gower Heritage Centre through ancient ash woodlands to reach this Stone Age cave. The chambers were used by hunters at the end of the last Ice Age and as a burial site during the Bronze Age. Nearby is Giant's Grave, an important Neolithic burial chamber.
❸ Parkmill

Mumbles

This quintessential Victorian seaside resort is the perfect tonic after a sightseeing overdose in Cardiff and Swansea. Potter around the boutiques, galleries and craft shops, pausing for an ice cream or coffee by the water's edge. The 244-m (800-ft) pier and medieval Oystermouth Castle are highlights of a visit.
Ⓦ www.mumblestic.co.uk

Oxwich Bay

Mighty dunes and tall cliffs add to the appeal of Oxwich Bay. Three km (2 miles) of clean sands and safe waters make the beach a top choice for families. Watersports enthusiasts catch the surf, while keen walkers follow the coast at low tide to Tor Bay and Three Cliffs Bay. A nature trail from the car park leads to the dunes, taking in the freshwater marshes, woodlands and coastal views.

Pennard Castle

Clinging to the cliff top and perched high above the Pennard Pill stream, this 12th-century castle's crumbling greystone towers afford giddy views of Three Cliffs Bay and Penmaen Burrows. A boardwalk and sandy paths lead down to the beach.

🄰 Pennard

Plantasia

Split into tropical, arid and humid climates, this giant glass pyramid in Swansea's city centre shelters rare and endangered species in its glasshouse, aquarium and vivarium. See cacti, cocoa trees and brightly coloured butterflies, or super-sized Giant African Snails.

🄰 Parc Tawe, Swansea 🄣 01792 474555 🄛 10.00–17.00. Admission charge

🔺 Mumbles is a lovely traditional seaside resort, complete with pier

Rhossili Bay

A smooth horseshoe-shaped bay backed by the Rhossili Downs, this beautiful spot is a mecca for surfers. For the best views, climb 200 m (656 ft) to the Rhossili Down Commons to spy the 5-km (3-mile) bay and Worm's Head promontory. Beware of undertows if you decide to take a dip here.

ⓐ National Trust Visitor Centre, Rhossili ❶ 01792 390707
🕐 10.30–17.30

Swansea Castle

Somewhat dwarfed by the modern BT Tower next to it, this was originally a Norman castle overlooking the River Tawe. During Victorian times, parts of the castle were used as a prison and town hall. Located in Swansea centre, the castle now stands testimony to the city that has sprung up around it.

ⓐ Castle Square, Swansea

Three Cliffs Bay

This bay is as scenic as they come, with a sweep of golden sand, thrashed by clear waters and three triangular cliffs rising dramatically above the shore. Spectacular views make it a climbing hot spot, but you can appreciate them on an gentle hike from Penmaen's sand dunes or Parkmill. If you walk beneath the cliffs, make sure you can get back – both the vista and the rip tides can be breathtaking!

Worm's Head

A National Trust Nature Reserve, this serpentine outcrop sits at the westernmost tip of the Gower Peninsula. While it's possible to walk the length of the 'worm', beware of the tides. Atlantic swells show no mercy towards foolhardy tourists, so if you want to play it safe and avoid getting stranded, soak up the views from Rhossili Bay.

ⓐ National Trust Visitor Centre, Rhossili ⓣ 01792 390707

ⓛ 10.30–17.30

CULTURE

Dylan Thomas Centre

Poetic souls are in their element at this centre dedicated to Swansea's literary hero Dylan Thomas. Located in a prime position

⬥ Beautiful Rhossili Bay is great for surfing

on Swansea's regenerated waterfront, the main exhibition captures
the poet's life and work with murals, readings and video screenings.
ⓐ Somerset Place, Swansea ❶ 01792 463980
ⓦ www.dylanthomas.org 🕐 10.00–16.30

Gower Heritage Centre

Set around a 12th-century watermill, the centre houses a rural-life
museum and gives guided tours through the corn and saw mill. A
must for families, there are playgrounds, puppet shows and animals
to keep children entertained.
ⓐ Parkmill ❶ 01792 371206 ⓦ www.gowerheritagecentre.co.uk
🕐 10.00–16.30. Admission charge

National Waterfront Museum

A landmark in Swansea's maritime quarter, this slate-and-glass
structure houses a world-class museum, with interactive exhibits
bringing Wales' industrial past to life. High-tech displays evoke the
Industrial Revolution, from the grime to the gold. Visitors experience
15 themes including work, landscape, coal and money. Keep an eye
open for the kinetic sculptures and virtual shop.
ⓐ Maritime Quarter, Swansea ❶ 01792 638950
ⓦ www.waterfrontmuseum.co.uk 🕐 10.00–17.00

Swansea Grand Theatre

With the grace and grandeur of yesteryear, Swansea's Victorian
theatre is home to the Ballet Russe, the UK's only Russian ballet
company. The huge auditorium stages performances from musicals
and modern dance to stand-up comedy and opera.
ⓐ Singleton Street ❶ 01792 475715
ⓦ www.swanseagrand.co.uk

Taliesin Arts Centre

Venture into Swansea's lesser-known cultural waters at this arts centre, part of the city's university. Independent films, innovative productions, contemporary art and Wales' largest collection of Egyptian artefacts make this a good choice.

ⓐ Swansea University, Singleton Park ⓣ 01792 602060
ⓦ www.taliesinartscentre.co.uk

RECREATION

Breakout Adventure

Thrills and most likely a few spills are on offer with this professional team. Activities range from canoeing to caving, coasteering and kayaking. ⓐ 26 Woodland Avenue, Swansea ⓣ 01792 584209
ⓦ www.breakout-adventure.org

Gower Coast Adventures

Skim Gower's coastline on the Sea Serpent, with a high-speed round trip to Three Cliffs Bay or Worm's Head. If you're lucky, you'll spy Atlantic Grey Seals and puffins around the rocks. ⓐ Knab Rock, Mumbles ⓣ 07866 250440 ⓦ www.gowercoastadventures.co.uk

Gower Surfing School

If you want to ride Wales' waves, Swansea's 4-star approved British Surfing School is ideal. The centre offers surfing courses for absolute beginners and advanced surfers. Equipment is provided.
ⓐ 6 Slade Road, Newton ⓣ 01792 386669 ⓦ www.surfgsd.com

Parc le Breos

Gallop along Gower with a professional guide. This riding centre in

Parkmill offers half-day and day rides, as well as weekend and week treks. Sturdy footwear and warm clothes are recommended.

ⓐ Parc-le-Breos House, Parkmill ☏ 01792 371636
ⓦ www.parc-le-breos.co.uk

RETAIL THERAPY

Lovespoon Gallery Buy a handcarved Welsh lovespoon in the Mumbles. Patricia Price's traditional tokens of affection are carved from a single piece of wood, with over 300 designs to choose from.
ⓐ 492 Mumbles Road ☏ 01792 360132 ⓦ www.lovespoons.co.uk
🕓 10.00–17.30 Mon–Sat, closed Sun

Mumbles Pottery Right on the Mumbles seafront, this ocean-themed shop is *the* place to pick up a handthrown, handpainted pot. Children can craft and paint their own. ⓐ 626 Mumbles Road ☏ 01792 361245 ⓦ www.mumblespottery.com 🕓 09.30–17.30 Mon–Sat, 09.30–16.00 Sun Feb–Dec

PJs Surf Shop
Want to tackle those waves? Kit yourself out with a board, wetsuit and a set of fins from this Llangennith shop.
ⓐ Llangennith ☏ 01792 386669 🕓 09.30–17.30

Swansea Market Fresh cockles, laverbread and organic fruits fill the stalls at central Swansea's covered market, the largest of its kind in Wales. This is a buzzing spot to shop for local produce and crafts under a glass roof. ⓐ Oxford Street, Swansea 🕓 08.30–17.00 Mon–Sat, closed Sun

THE GOWER PENINSULA & SWANSEA BAY

The Green Gallery Fine art inspired by local landscapes graces the walls at Rhossili's gallery. Even if you can't afford an original, this is window shopping with a cultural twist. ⓐ Rhossili ☏ 01792 391190 ⓦ www.thegreengallery.co.uk ⏱ 09.00–17.00

TAKING A BREAK

Castellamare £ Overlooking picturesque Bracelet Bay, this Italian restaurant is decorated with the work of local artists.
ⓐ Bracelet Bay ☏ 01792 369408 ⓦ www.castellamare.co.uk
⏱ 10.00–23.00

Surfside Café £ The perfect pit stop for a coffee, panini or real dairy ice cream, this chilled café in Caswell Bay has moreish sea views.
ⓐ Caswell Bay ☏ 01792 368368 ⏱ 09.30–18.00

The Bay Bistro & Café £ This cosy bistro and café in Rhossili serves snacks and light lunches such as jacket potatoes, paninis and home-made shepherd's pie. ⓐ Rhossili ☏ 01792 390519 ⏱ 09.00–18.00

▲ *Treat yourself to tea and cakes in one of Mumbles' many cafés*

Three Cliffs Coffee Shop £ Open 364 days a year, this coffee shop near Three Cliffs Bay serves light meals using Welsh produce, plus cakes and hot drinks. ⓐ 68 Southgate Road, Southgate ⓣ 01792 233230 ⓦ www.threecliffs.com ⓛ 09.00–18.00

Verdi's Café £ Pause for a cappuccino, pizza or one of 30 varieties of fresh ice cream at this excellent Italian café on the Mumbles seafront. ⓐ Knab Rock, Mumbles ⓣ 01792 369135 ⓛ 10.00–21.00

Welcome to Town £ Opposite the village church in Llanrhidian, this charming 17th-century cottage serves well-prepared Welsh fare. Feast on a lunch of laverbread and Black beef beneath the beams. ⓐ Llanrhidian ⓣ 01792 390015 ⓛ 12.00–14.00, 19.00–21.00 Tues–Sat, 12.00–14.00 Sun, closed Mon

AFTER DARK

Bay View Bar £ Swansea Bay meets Siam at this bar serving Thai food fresh from the wok. Come here for lunch, dinner or to relax with a drink by the open fire. ⓐ 400 Oystermouth Road, Swansea ⓣ 01792 652610 ⓦ www.bayviewbar.co.uk ⓛ 12.00–15.00, 18.00–22.00 Mon–Sat, 12.00–16.00 Sun

Truffle £ The set three-course menu at this North African-inspired restaurant offers great value. Try fiery chilli peppers stuffed with feta and aubergine tagine with couscous. You can bring a bottle and there's no corkage fee. ⓐ 68 Brynmor Road, Swansea ⓣ 01792 547246 ⓦ www.truffle-swansea.co.uk ⓛ 19.00–23.00 Tues–Sat, closed Sun & Mon

698 £–££ This trendy newcomer to the Mumbles scene is definitely a name not a number, combining black leather chairs with exposed brickwork. Flavours range from Tuscan white bean soup to braised Welsh lamb. ⊕ 698 Mumbles Road ☎ 01792 361616 ⓦ www.698.uk.com ⏰ 10.00–23.00

Bouchon de Rossi ££ Laid-back and friendly, this French café and bistro scores points for its eclectic menu and efficient staff. Try garlicky mussels or beer-battered cod. ⊕ 217 Oxford Street, Swansea ☎ 01792 655780 ⏰ 11.00–14.30, 18.00–22.00 Tues–Fri, 11.00–22.00 Sat, closed Sun & Mon

Chelsea Café ££ Head for Swansea's café quarter to this hip place, with its clean colours, wooden floors and original art. Head chef Mat Hole uses organic, local produce such as fresh cockles and Gower lamb. ⊕ 17 St Mary's Street, Swansea ☎ 01792 464068 ⓦ www.chelseacafe.co.uk ⏰ 12.00–14.30, 19.00–23.30 Tues–Sat, closed Sun & Mon

Fairyhill £££ Blow the budget on 5-star cuisine at this vine-clad 18th-century manor set in 10 hectares (24 acres) of grounds. Specialities include seared scallops and filo tart of vine tomatoes with local goat's cheese. ⊕ Reynoldston ☎ 01792 390139 ⓦ www.fairyhill.net ⏰ 12.30–14.00, 19.30–21.00

ACCOMMODATION

Bank Farm Leisure Park £ A few steps from the beach, this 30-hectare (75-acre) campsite has views to Port Eynon Bay. Plus points include the on-site bar, heated outdoor pool, children's

playground and grocery shop. ⓐ Bank Farm Leisure Park, Horton
ⓣ 01792 390228 ⓦ www.bankfarmleisure.co.uk

Nicholaston Farm Caravan & Camping £ Just off the Swansea to Port
Eynon road, this campsite on a working farm has pick-your-own
fruit. Spacious pitches on the meadow overlook Tor Bay, and nearby
Cefn Bryn hill affords sweeping views over Gower. ⓐ Penmaen
ⓣ 01792 371209 ⓦ www.nicholastonfarm.co.uk

Pitton Cross £ Pitch a tent at this peaceful site with sea views. It's an
ideal base for coastal walks to Worm's Head and Rhossili Bay, with
clean facilities, a laundry room, shop and play area. ⓐ Pitton Cross,
Rhossili ⓣ 01792 390593

Barlands Cottage ££ A quiet 250-year-old cottage in the Bishopston
Valley, this B&B exudes country charm. Snug en-suite rooms
decorated in warm colours have TV and tea-making facilities.
ⓐ Old Kittle Road, Bishopston ⓣ 01792 232615
ⓦ www.barlandscottage.co.uk

Coast House ££ This family-run guesthouse on the Mumbles
seafront offers good value. Enjoy clean and comfy en-suite rooms,
some with views of Swansea Bay. ⓐ 708 Mumbles Road
ⓣ 01792 368702 ⓦ www.thecoasthouse.co.uk

Highmead B&B ££ Coastal walks, sandy beaches and Port Eynon are
on the doorstep of this 4-star B&B. All rooms have sea views and
there's a lounge where you can unwind after a long hike.
ⓐ Overton, Port Eynon ⓣ 01792 390300
ⓦ www.highmead-gower.co.uk

King Arthur Hotel ££ Legend has it that this is a great place to stay on Gower. The country inn lives up to its reputation, with spotless, spacious rooms overlooking gardens. A bonus is the pub's restaurant serving hearty Welsh food and real ales. ➋ Higher Green, Reynoldston ➊ 01792 390775

Little Haven Guesthouse ££ This first-rate Oxwich B&B has homely en-suite rooms, a heated outdoor pool and a terrace. The beach is just a short stroll away. ➊ Oxwich Bay ➊ 01792 390940 ➍ www.littlehavenoxwich.co.uk

North Gower Hotel ££ Located in gardens and overlooking the Loughor Estuary, this olde-worlde hotel in Llanrhidian has 18 well-kept rooms with mod cons. There's a good restaurant and bar on site. ➋ Llanrhidian ➊ 01792 390042 ➍ www.northgowerhotel.co.uk

Parc Le Breos ££ You'll feel like lord of the manor at this grand 19th-century hunting lodge in 28 hectares (70 acres) of grounds. A 1.6-km (1-mile) drive through woods and meadows brings you to the lodge, with its log fires, carp pond and terrace. Combine your stay with a canter along the coast. ➌ Parc-Le-Breos House, Parkmill ➊ 01792 371636 ➍ www.parc-le-breos.co.uk

The Dragon Hotel ££ For those that prefer retro to rustic, this modern and central Swansea hotel offers affordable indulgence in Zen-style rooms. After hiking or biking Gower, relax with a massage at the health club or cocktails at the bar. ➌ Kingsway Circle, Swansea ➊ 08704 299848 ➍ www.dragon-hotel.co.uk

OUT OF TOWN

Brecon Beacons National Park

Spanning 1,347 sq km (520 sq miles), the Brecon Beacons National Park's raw beauty and sense of solitude lures independent travellers. Above the ground, open moors and dense woodlands are dominated by limestone crags and lofty peaks. Below the ground, chambers, caves and mines interweave. This is prime hiking, biking and camping territory just an hour's drive north of Cardiff.

GETTING THERE

While a car makes getting to remote corners of the national park easier, Cardiff has good public transport connections to the main towns. Sixty Six Coaches operates the frequent X43 service, linking Cardiff bus station to Merthyr Tydfil, Brecon, Crickhowell and Abergavenny; and Arriva Trains (☎ 08457 48 49 50 ⓦ www.arrivatrainswales.co.uk) runs an hourly service from Cardiff to Merthyr Tydfil and a half-hourly train from Cardiff to Abergavenny.

SIGHTS & ATTRACTIONS

Beacons Horseshoe

If you've got a head for heights, this 14-km (9-mile) hike could appeal. The challenging ridge walk encompasses the Brecon Beacon's three highest peaks: Pen y Fan (886 m/2,906 ft), Corn Du (873 m/2,864 ft) and Cribyn (795 m/2,608 ft). Some parts are steep, but trekkers are rewarded with sweeping views of peaks, lakes and valleys. Allow 7 hours, pick up a map and check weather conditions before heading out.

❷ Cwm Gedi Training Camp car park (off the B4601)

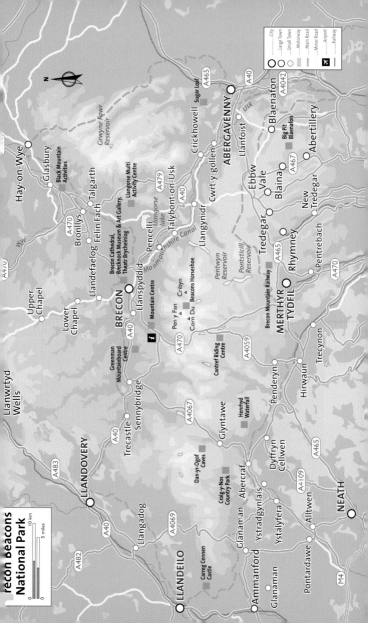

Big Pit Blaenafon

Part of the UNESCO World Heritage Site of Blaenafon, Big Pit is an eye-opening attraction offering free underground tours of a real coal mine. After kitting up with a helmet and cap lamp, visitors descend 90 m (295 ft) down the mineshaft in a pit cage. Don't miss the colliery buildings, mining galleries and Pithead Baths.

ⓐ Blaenafon ☎ 01495 790311 ⓦ www.museumwales.ac.uk

🕒 09.30–17.00; underground tours 10.00–15.30

Brecon Mountain Railway

Too tired to climb every mountain? Let a steam train do the hard work and enjoy views over the Taf Fechan Reservoir and the Brecon

⬤ Let the train take the strain on the Brecon Mountain Railway

Beacons' trio of peaks: *Pen y Fan*, *Corn Du* and *Cribyn*.

ⓐ Pant Station, Merthyr Tydfil ☎ 01685 722988 🌐 www.brecon mountainrailway.co.uk 🕐 10.00–16.30 Apr–Oct. Admission charge

Craig-y-Nos Country Park

This peaceful country park in the upper Swansea valley is a patchwork of lakes, meadows, rivers and forests. A network of trails weaves through the park and it's a great spot for a picnic in summer.

ⓐ Brecon Road, Penycae ☎ 01639 730395 🕐 10.00–dusk

Dan-yr-Ogof Caves

Lose yourself in an underground labyrinth of chambers, passages and caves at these award-winning caves. Glimpse yawning Cathedral Cave and spooky Bone Cave, where 3,000-year-old skeletons were discovered. The site also features a reconstructed Iron Age village, conservation museum and farm.

ⓐ Dan-yr-Ogof ☎ 01639 730801 🌐 www.dan-yr-ogof-showcaves.co.uk 🕐 10.00–15.00 Apr–Oct. Admission charge

Henrhyd Waterfall

Water cascades 27 m (89 ft) at the highest falls in the Brecon Beacons. Tucked away in a green gorge, the striking waterfall can be reached by taking the steep footpath through the woods.

ⓐ National Trust car park, near Coelbren (off the A4221)

Llangorse Lake

This nutrient-rich lake is a haven for wildlife including yellow water lilies and dragonflies. Flanked by reeds and willow woods, the tranquil lake was carved out by glacial movement during the last Ice Age.

ⓐ Llangorse

Mountain Centre

Eight km (5 miles) southwest of Brecon, this helpful visitor centre has plenty of information, maps, books and an exhibition on the national park. There are great views of Pen y Fan from here and you can recharge your batteries with a light lunch in the café.

ⓐ Libanus ① 01874 623366 ⓦ www.brecon-beacons.com
🕐 09.30–18.00 (summer); 09.30–16.30 (winter)

Sugar Loaf

Climb to the narrow ridge of this conical 596-m (1,955-ft) mountain for 360° views of the Bristol Channel and Malvern Hills. To the north of Abergavenny, the uphill trek through moors and woodlands begins in the car park that can be reached on a narrow lane just off the A40.

CULTURE

Brecknock Museum & Art Gallery

Housed in a Victorian shire hall, this intriguing museum and art gallery traces local and natural history, with displays on Welsh life, industry and crafts. Highlights include the huge collection of Welsh lovespoons.

ⓐ Captain's Walk, Brecon ① 01874 624121 🕐 10.00–17.00 Mon–Sat, 12.00–17.00 Sun, Apr–Sept

Brecon Cathedral

Explore 900 years of history at Brecon's beautiful cathedral, dating back to 1094. Admire Britain's largest Norman font before visiting the heritage centre and craft shop in the 16th-century tithe barn.

@ Cathedral Close, Brecon ☎ 01874 623857
Ⓦ www.breconcathedral.org.uk 🕐 08.30–18.00

Carreg Cennen Castle

Clinging to a limestone crag above the River Cennen, this grey stone
fortress is worth the climb. The romantic 13th-century castle is one
of Wales' most impressive, with giddy views of the Black Mountain.
@ Trapp, near Llandeilo 🕐 09.30–16.30 Oct–Mar; 09.30–20.30
Apr–Sept

Theatr Brycheiniog

Brecon's modern theatre stages first-rate concerts and performances,
welcoming leading companies to the stage such as The Royal
National Theatre and BBC National Orchestra of Wales. The eclectic

▲ *There's plenty to do and see in the pretty market town of Brecon*

line up stretches from jazz and rock to musicals, ballet and comedy.

🅐 Canal Wharf, Brecon 🕾 01874 611622

🕒 Box office: 10.00–17.00

RECREATION

Black Mountain Activities

Adrenaline-fuelled activities are a major draw in the Black
Mountains. This professional team offers outdoor thrills including
rock climbing, high rope courses, gorge walking, caving, potholing
and kayaking. Day courses for beginners are available.

🅐 Three Cocks, Brecon 🕾 01497 847897

🅦 www.blackmountain.co.uk

Cantref Riding Centre

A top address for horse riding in the Brecon Beacons, this centre's
treks cater to all levels and include half-day rides to the foothills,
plus day rides to the mountains and woodlands. An on-site
farmhouse and bunkhouse make this a good base.

🅐 Cantref, Brecon 🕾 01874 665223 🅦 www.cantref.com

Greenman Mountainboard Centre

Join the mountainboarders to hit the Beacons' slopes at the
Penpont Estate. The centre provides training on negotiating
carving runs and free slopes. Hill riders are taken to the summit
on a tractor – a slow uphill climb followed by a speedy
downhill descent!

🅐 Penpont Estate 🕾 01874 636202

🅦 www.greenman-mountainboard.co.uk 🕒 11.00–18.00 Sat & Sun,
Apr–Oct; closed Mon–Fri

Llangorse Multi Activity Centre

Those after adventure in high doses will not be disappointed at this multi-award-winning centre. Get wet and muddy dingle scrambling, traversing waterfalls, crawling through pipes or swinging through the treetops. It's also Wales' biggest climbing and riding centre.

ⓐ Gilfach Farm, Llangorse ☎ 01874 658272 🌐 www.activityuk.com
🕙 09.00–17.00. Admission charge

Taff Trail

Linking Brecon to Cardiff Bay, this 89-km (55-mile) trail is a magnet to hikers and mountain bikers. A network of railway, canal and forest paths takes in highlights such as Castell Coch, Merthyr Tydfil and the Talybont Reservoir. Details on shorter hikes are given on the Taff Trail website.

🌐 www.tafftrail.org.uk

🔺 *Kayaking in the Black Mountains*

RETAIL THERAPY

Beacons Crafts This workshop and studios in central Brecon
showcases Welsh arts and crafts, from woodwork to ceramics,
jewellery, textiles, candles and glasswork. ⓐ Bethel Square, Brecon
ⓣ 01874 625706 ⓦ www.beaconscrafts.co.uk ⓛ 10.00–17.00 Mon–Sat,
closed Sun

Brecon Farmers' Market Fresh local produce fills the stalls at this
market held in Brecon on the second Saturday of the month. Shop
for organic vegetables, fruit, cheese and chutney to the sound of live
jazz or classical music. ⓐ Brecon ⓣ 01874 610008 ⓛ 10.00–14.00 Sat,
closed Sun–Fri

Sugar Loaf Vineyards Sitting in Sugar Loaf's shadow, these
peaceful vineyards overlooking the Usk Valley offer wine tastings
and tours. Sample zingy whites and heavy reds before you buy.
ⓐ Pentre Lane, Abergavenny ⓣ 01873 853066
ⓦ www.sugarloafvineyards.co.uk ⓛ 11.00–16.00 Tues–Sat,
12.00–16.00 Sun, Mar–Dec, closed Mon

TAKING A BREAK

Llanfaes £ Dairy ice cream made fresh on the premises is the
purpose of a visit to this parlour. Satisfy your sweet tooth with one
of 42 flavours, like pink grapefruit, chocolate orange and Turkish
delight. The best thing is that you can see the ice cream being made
through the viewing window.
ⓐ 19 Bridge Street, Brecon ⓣ 01874 625892 ⓦ www.llanfaesdairy.net
ⓛ 10.00–18.00

Pilgrim Tea Rooms £ Beneath Brecon Cathedral's cloisters, you'll find this award-winning gem of a tea room. Janet Williams serves light lunches and afternoon teas using local ingredients. Enjoy a warming lamb casserole, freshly baked flapjack, or pre-book a picnic hamper for lunch in the hills. ⓐ Brecon Cathedral Close ⓣ 01874 610610 ⓦ www.pilgrims-tearooms.co.uk ⓒ 10.00–17.00 (summer); 10.00–16.00 (winter)

The Old Barn Tearoom £ Pause at this atmospheric 18th-century barn to the north of the Taff valley to try the delicious home-made cakes with a pot of tea. You'll find the tearoom on the mountain road between Talybont-on-Usk and Merthyr Tydfil. ⓐ Ystradgynwyn ⓣ 01685 383358 ⓒ 11.00–17.00 Wed–Mon, closed Tues

AFTER DARK

Roberto's £ An intimate feel and Italian dishes cooked with finesse tempt at this laid-back trattoria in Brecon. It's a pleasant spot for dinner after a long day's sightseeing. Booking is recommended. ⓐ The Old Sorting Office, St Mary's Street, Brecon ⓣ 01874 611880 ⓒ 18.00–22.00

The Barn at Brynich £ This converted 17th-century hay barn scores top points for its views of the Beacons from the courtyard, roaring fire and organic local produce. Sample specialities like Welsh stilton tartlets and tender Brecknockshire lamb. ⓐ Brynich ⓣ 01874 623480 ⓦ www.barn-restaurant.co.uk ⓒ 10.00–23.00 Tues–Sun, closed Mon

The Dragon Hotel £ The imaginative menu ranges from Welsh Black steaks to mussels in Thai green curry at this 17th-century hotel in

Crickhowell. ⓐ High Street, Crickhowell ❶ 01873 810362
Ⓦ www.dragonhotel.co.uk ❹ 18.30–21.30 Mon–Sat, closed Sun

The Felin Fach Griffin £ Head chef Ricardo Van Ede won a Michelin
star at the age of 21. His foodie philosophy is simple: eat, drink,
sleep (and be merry). Expect home-grown vegetables and high-
quality local produce like Welsh venison and Portland crab to land on
your plate. ⓐ Felin Fach ❶ 01874 620111 Ⓦ www.eatdrinksleep.ltd.uk
❹ 12.30–14.30, 19.00–21.00 Tues–Sun; 19.00–21.00 Mon

The White Hart £ If it's cold outside, warm by the log fires in the bar
and beamed dining room at this 16th-century coaching inn. Welsh
specialities like roast duck with sloe gin are staples on the menu.
In summer, sample real ales in the beer garden. ⓐ Talybont-on-Usk
❶ 01873 810473 ❹ 12.00–14.30, 18.00–21.30 Mon–Sat, 12.00–14.30,
18.30–21.00 Sun

Nantyffin Cider Mill Inn ££ Looking pretty in pink, this award-
winning inn at the foot of the Black Mountains is set around a
16th-century cider mill. The characterful restaurant combines
fresh flavours like Cornish mussels with cider and leeks.
ⓐ Brecon Road ❶ 01873 810775 Ⓦ www.cidermill.co.uk
❹ 12.00–14.30, 18.00–21.30 Tues–Sun, closed Mon

The Usk Inn ££ A welcome break, this award-winning village inn
prides itself on seafood and traditional Welsh fare. Tuck into crab
fishcakes, garlicky mussels or Caecrwn pork in the bistro, or kick back
with a pint of real ale on the terrace. ⓐ Talybont-on-Usk
❶ 01874 676251 Ⓦ www.uskinn.co.uk ❹ Restaurant: 18.30–21.30; Bar:
11.00–23.00

ACCOMMODATION

Anchorage Caravan Park £ Pitch a tent at this leafy family-run campsite, with panoramic views of the nearby Black Mountains. Excellent facilities include a shop, post office, laundry room, hair salon, TV lounge and play area. ❷ Bronllys ❶ 01874 711246 ⓦ www.anchoragecp.co.uk

Canal Barn Bunkhouse £ Popular with hikers and cyclists, this bunkhouse is 5-star roughing it. Tucked away in rural Trecastle, the oak-beamed cow shed offers comfy beds, plenty of hot water, and a communal kitchen and dining room. A bridle path leads to Roman ruins. Bring your own sleeping bag and towel. ❷ Ynysmarchog Farm, Trecastle ❶ 01874 638000 ⓦ www.bunkhousewales.co.uk

Lakeside £ Set in open countryside, this peaceful site is just a short stroll from Llangorse Lake and is a good base to explore the Beacons. Guest facilities include a clubhouse, shop and café. You can hire boats, canoes and windsurfing equipment here. ❷ Llangorse ❶ 01874 658226 ⓦ www.lakeside-holidays.net ❸ Apr–Oct

Pencelli Castle £ This multi-award-winning site is set in a tranquil spot 6 km (4 miles) from Brecon. Walk the highest peaks, hire mountain bikes, or launch a canoe on the canal that runs through the meadow. The site is also a WiFi hotspot. ❷ Pencelli ❶ 01874 665451 ⓦ www.pencelli-castle.co.uk

YHA Brecon £ Not just another bog-standard hostel, this rambling house just a couple of miles outside Brecon has real Victorian charm.

First-rate facilities include a barbecue area, common room, cycle store, kitchen and laundry. ⓐ Groesffordd ⓣ 0870 770 5718 ⓦ www.yha.org.uk

Blaencar Farm ££ Escape to the country at this working farm. All exposed beams, stonework and heavy oak doors, the traditional farmhouse serves a hearty breakfast. The friendly owners can help with maps, storage and packed lunches. ⓐ Sennybridge ⓣ 01874 636610 ⓦ www.blaencar.co.uk

Castle of Brecon Hotel ££ Sitting on Brecon Castle's remains, this whitewashed 18th-century coaching inn rises above the town with superb views of the River Usk valley. The elegant rooms have TV, coffee-making facilities and direct dial phone. ⓐ The Castle Square, Brecon ⓣ 01874 624611 ⓦ www.breconcastle.co.uk

Llwyn Onn Guest House ££–£££ This country house overlooking the Llwyn Onn Reservoir is a good base for the Taff Trail. Smart rooms have views over gardens or woodland and you can use the nearby spa for free. ⓐ Llwyn Onn, near Merthyr Tydfil ⓣ 01685 384384 ⓦ www.llwynonn.co.uk

Nant Ddu £££ If you're craving creature comforts, this spa retreat is just the ticket. Stylish rooms look out on lawns, fields and forest. Snuggle up by the log fire in the bar or unwind in the hydro-spa and sauna. ⓐ Cwm Taf, near Merthyr Tydfil ⓣ 01685 379111 ⓦ www.nant-ddu-lodge.co.uk

---

▶ *Saturday shoppers on Queen Street*

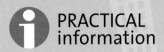

Directory

GETTING THERE

By air

Many international airlines serve Cardiff with direct and frequent flights to major European cities including Paris, Brussels and Amsterdam, as well as Vancouver and Toronto in Canada. These include:

bmibaby ☎ 0870 264 2229 🖝 www.bmibaby.com

Excel ☎ 0870 169 0169 🖝 www.xl.com

KLM ☎ 0870 507 4074 🖝 www.klm.com

Thomsonfly ☎ 0870 1900 737 🖝 www.thomsonfly.com

Zoom ☎ 0870 240 0055 🖝 www.flyzoom.com

🛈 Many people are aware that air travel emits CO_2, which contributes to climate change. You may be interested in the possibility of lessening the environmental impact of your flight through the charity Climate Care, which offsets your CO_2 by funding environmental projects around the world. 🖝 www.climatecare.org

By rail

Cardiff Central station has excellent rail connections to major cities across the UK such as London, Bristol and Birmingham. The following companies operate a regular service:

Arriva Trains ☎ 08457 48 49 50 🖝 www.arrivatrainswales.co.uk

First Great Western ☎ 08457 000 125 🖝 www.firstgreatwestern.co.uk

Virgin ☎ 0870 789 1234 🖝 www.virgintrains.co.uk

By bus

Travelling by bus is perhaps the cheapest way to reach other UK destinations like London, Bristol, Oxford and Glasgow. National

Express and Megabus offer some great deals if you're flexible about when you travel.

Megabus ☎ 0900 160 0900 Ⓦ www.megabus.com
National Express ☎ 08705 808080 Ⓦ www.nationalexpress.com

Driving
The roads and motorways are good and fast through Wales, and with a clear run on the M4 you can drive from London to Cardiff in 2 hours 30 minutes. If possible, it's best to avoid driving during rush hour (08.00–09.30 and 17.00–18.30) when motorways can be congested. It takes around 3 hours and 30 minutes to reach Dover, where there are regular ferries to Calais in France.

ENTRY FORMALITIES
Entry and visa requirements for Wales are the same as for the rest of the UK. EU, US, Canadian, Australian, South African and New Zealand citizens must have a valid passport, but do not need a visa.

ⓘ Visitors from other countries may need a visa to enter the UK and should contact their consulate or embassy before departure. More information on visas is available at Ⓦ www.ukvisas.gov.uk

MONEY
The national currency is the British pound (GBP), which is divided into 100 pence. One British pound is roughly equivalent to 1.80 US dollars or 1.45 euros.

ATM cashpoint machines are plentiful in the city centre and accept most major credit and debit cards including Visa and MasterCard. Alternatively, many large supermarkets such as Tesco and Sainsbury's offer cashback at the checkout.

Most restaurants, hotels and department stores accept Visa, MasterCard and American Express. Many shops, especially in areas frequented by tourists, also accept card payments.

HEALTH, SAFETY & CRIME

Wales is generally a safe place to visit and there are no particular health risks. No vaccinations or health certificates are required and the tap water is safe to drink.

Health

Pharmacies stock medication to treat minor ailments. They usually open 08.30–18.00 Mon–Sat and 11.00–17.00 Sun. Dispensaries at major supermarkets often stay open later.

The British National Health Service (NHS) offers free emergency care to EU citizens and nationals from countries with reciprocal health agreements with the UK, including Australia and New Zealand.

There is a charge for routine medical care. Travellers from other countries such as the US, Canada and South Africa should invest in a good health insurance policy.

Further information is given on the Department of Health website ⓦ www.dh.gov.uk

Safety & crime

Cardiff has a low crime rate and travel is generally safe here, even for lone travellers. However, it's advisable to take good care of your belongings and be aware of your surroundings. The general rules apply about not carrying large sums of money, or drawing unwanted attention with expensive jewellery and cameras. If you are the victim of a crime or other emergency, you should inform the police immediately by calling 999. See Emergencies (page 156) for further details and listings.

OPENING HOURS

Shops Most shops in Cardiff open 09.00–17.30 Mon–Sat and 10.00–16.00 Sun. Some of the centre's malls and department stores open later on Thursdays.

Attractions The majority of Cardiff's key attractions open 10.00–17.00 daily. Some open later during the summer months.

Banks Banks generally open 09.00–17.00 Mon–Sat, although some smaller branches may close at the weekend.

TOILETS

There are a number of attended public toilets in the city centre that are clean and well maintained, as well as automatic conveniences. You'll find attended toilets at Hayes Island, St David's, Wood Street and Kingsway. Most facilities open 07.15–23.45 daily.

CHILDREN

A green and child-friendly city, Cardiff appeals to families with its leafy parks, fairy-tale castles, interactive museums and laid-back restaurants. There's plenty to keep children entertained, from playgrounds where they can let off excess energy to safe and sandy beaches on the nearby Glamorgan Heritage Coast, where kids can paddle or hunt for fossils.

Dining Children are welcome in most cafés and restaurants, some offering special menus to suit little appetites. Relaxed TGI Fridays on Newport Road is an excellent choice (☏ 029 2046 0123), as is The

Allensbank on Wedal Road (☎ 029 2061 7054) with a play area to keep tots amused. In Mermaid Quay, Demiros (☎ 029 2049 1882) has great pizza, fair prices and a gooey chocolate fountain that kids love.

Playgrounds Kids can play freely on the pirate ships in Cardiff Bay's sandy playground. There is also an adventure playground in Roath Park.

Quick change There are nappy-changing facilities in most of Cardiff's major department stores, such as Debenhams and bhs, and also in Cardiff Bay's clean public toilets and some attractions including Techniquest.

Some child-friendly places
- **Barry Island Pleasure Park** When the sun shines, take your kids to the seaside. A 20-minute ride from Cardiff, Barry Island's theme park draws families with its log flume, rollercoasters and giant pirate ship. ➌ Barry Island ☎ 01446 732844 ⓦ www.barryisland.com ⌚ 12.00–19.00 Sat & Sun, closed Mon–Fri

TRAVELLING WITH CHILDREN

❶ Up to three children under five years of age travel free with Cardiff Bus when accompanied by a fare-paying adult, while those aged 5 to 15 pay a child fare.

❶ Arriva Trains offers reductions on child and family tickets.

❶ Kids under 16 years of age enjoy half-price travel on the Cardiff Cat waterbus service.

▶ *Kids love the statues on the waterfront at Cardiff Bay*

- **National Museum & Gallery** Kids love the Evolution of Wales, tracing the country's history back millions of years to the age of dinosaurs and woolly mammoths. ⓐ Cathays Park ☎ 029 2039 7951 ⓕ 029 2057 3321 ⓦ www.nmgw.ac.uk ⏰ 10.00–17.00 Tues–Sun, closed Mon

- **Red Dragon Centre** Keep boredom at bay with a visit to this leisure complex, featuring a 12-screen UCI cinema, 26-lane bowling alley and diner-style restaurants serving children's favourite foods. ⓐ Hemingway Road ☎ 029 2025 6261 ⓦ www.thereddragoncentre.com

- **Techniquest** Children can get to grips with science at this hands-on discovery museum and test out 160 interactive exhibits, from firing a rocket to launching a hot-air balloon, experimenting in the laboratory or studying stars in the planetarium. ⓐ Stuart Street ☎ 029 2047 5475 ⓦ www.tquest.org.uk ⏰ 09.30–16.30 Mon–Fri, 10.30–17.00 Sat & Sun. Admission charge

COMMUNICATIONS
Phones
BT public telephone boxes are widely available in Cardiff and accept coins (10p, 20p, 50p and £1), phonecards and occasionally credit and debit cards. To phone Cardiff, dial 00 44 for the UK, then 29 (for Cardiff) followed by the eight-digit number. To phone out of Wales, dial 00 followed by the country code and the local number.

UK Directory Enquiries ☎ 118 500
International UK Directory Enquiries ☎ 118 505

Post

Stamps are sold in post offices and some newsagents. It costs 44p to send a standard letter or postcard to Europe, and 50p to send it to North America, Australia, New Zealand and South Africa.

The postal service in Wales is quick and efficient. There are a number of branches dotted throughout the city – including those in Churchill Way and Moira Place – as well as the main post office on Hills Street, which also has a bureau de change and shop.
ⓐ 2 Hills Street ① 029 2022 7305 ⓦ www.postoffice.co.uk
🕐 09.00–17.30 Mon–Sat, closed Sun

Internet

Cardiff has a handful of Internet cafés, although things are moving more towards WiFi these days. There are some good, cheap options in the city centre, where you'll pay around £1 for an hour online.

AGS Cyber Lounge Just outside of the city centre, this laid-back Internet café is a firm favourite among Cardiff's student population.
ⓐ 178 Whitechurch Road ① 029 2052 1800 ⓦ www.the-cyberlounge.co.uk 🕐 10.30–21.00 Mon–Fri, 10.30–19.00 Sat, 13.00–19.00 Sun

Cardiff Central Library If you want to surf for free, head for this library. Just off Queen Street, Wales' largest public library has over 60 PCs offering high-speed Internet access. There is a small charge for print-outs and floppy discs. ⓐ Frederick Street
① 029 2038 2116 🕐 09.00–18.00 Mon–Fri, 09.30–17.30 Sat, closed Sun

ELECTRICITY

The electrical system in Wales is very reliable. It is 240 volts AC, 50 Hz. Square three-pin plugs are standard.

TRAVELLERS WITH DISABILITIES

Cardiff caters well for those with disabilities and has come a long way to becoming wheelchair-accessible. Many of the city's modern facilities, attractions and public buildings have been thoughtfully designed with disabled visitors in mind, often featuring wheelchair ramps, low-level lift buttons and accessible toilets.

As most of the major sights group in the compact and flat city centre, it is generally easy to get around. Running a frequent service from Cardiff Central station to Cardiff Bay, the Bay Xpress bus is wheelchair-accessible. For more details contact Cardiff Bus (☏ 0870 608 2608 Ⓦ www.cardiffbus.com).

Many of Cardiff's key venues and attractions offer reduced entry for disabled visitors. These include St David's Hall and the New Theatre, with level floors and ramp access to the foyer. St Fagans National History Museum, the National Museum & Gallery and Techniquest are also fully accessible. The Millennium Stadium has special viewing platforms holding up to 200 wheelchair spectators.

While many restaurants display the disabled symbol, check before you visit them whether they have accessible toilet facilities. Good choices are trendy Salt restaurant and bar in Mermaid Quay and The Yard in The Old Brewery Quarter.

FURTHER INFORMATION
Cardiff Visitor Centre

In the heart of the capital, Cardiff's main tourist information centre provides information on local attractions, an accommodation booking service and a left-luggage facility. ➌ The Old Library, The Hayes ☎ 08701 211258 🅕 029 2066 8750 Ⓦ www.cardiff.gov.uk ✉ visitor@cardiff.gov.uk 🕐 09.30–18.00 Mon–Sat, 10.00–16.00 Sun

Cardiff Bay Visitor Centre

This futuristic visitor centre is an attraction in its own right. The award-winning design built of steel and plywood is in the shape of a giant telescope. Step inside to take in a free exhibition and admire views of the bay. Tourist information and maps are available. ➊ Harbour Drive ☎ 029 2046 3833 Ⓦ www.cardiffharbour.com 🕐 09.00–18.00 Mon–Sat, 10.30–18.00 Sun (summer); 09.00–18.00 Mon–Sat, 10.30–17.00 Sun (winter)

Visit Wales

Well designed and illustrated, this site is an invaluable tool for those travelling to Wales. As well as giving details on specific areas, visitors can search for places to stay, attractions, heritage, history and events. Brochures can be ordered online. The site lists tourist information centres across Wales. Ⓦ www.visitwales.com

FURTHER READING

Collected Poems, 1934–53 by Dylan Thomas (published by Everyman) Brush up on your knowledge of the works of Wales' most famous poet, Dylan Thomas.

Food Wales by Colin Pressdee (published by Graffeg) Find out more about specialities, shops, markets and restaurants in Wales.

Walk The Brecon Beacons by Bob Greaves (published by Discovery Walking Guides) This definitive guide to walking the Brecon Beacons features OS maps and a wide range of walks for beginners to experts.

Emergencies

EMERGENCY NUMBERS:
The following are free nationwide emergency numbers:

Police, fire and ambulance ❶ 999
European emergency number ❶ 112 (This is the standard SOS
number in all EU countries. The operator will connect you to the
service you need.)

❶ When you dial the UK emergency services number 999:
- ask for the service you require
- give details of where you are, what the emergency is and the
  number of the phone you are using.

POLICE
Police officers in Wales wear dark blue uniforms and a conical
helmet. The Cardiff Central Police Station in Cathays Park deals
with enquiries.
❷ King Edward VII Avenue ❶ 029 2022 2111

MEDICAL EMERGENCIES
Should you need emergency care, call 999 or 112 and ask for an
ambulance. The Accident and Emergency Department is at the
University Hospital of Wales in Heath Park (❶ 029 2074 7747).
Listings of doctors, some operating a 24-hour call-out service, can be
found in *Yellow Pages*.

Pharmacies usually open 08.30–18.00 Mon–Sat and 11.00–17.00
Sun. Dispensaries at major supermarkets often stay open later. For
over-the-counter and prescription medications, Boots the Chemist

has a number of branches across Cardiff, including the central
branch on Queen St ☎ 029 2023 1291

CONSULATES & EMBASSIES

Embassies and consulates dealing with passport and visa issues are
based in London.

ℹ️ For country-specific enquiries, contact the Foreign and
Commonwealth Office (☎ 020 7008 8438 ⓦ www.ukvisas.gov.uk).

🔺 *A Welsh dragon looks out over the city from the top of City Hall*

The publishers would like to thank the following individuals and organisations for supplying their copyright photos for this book:
Neil Setchfield: all photos except pages 44, 76, 127 Meghan Hurst

Copy editor: Sandra Stafford
Proofreader: Emma Sangster

Send your thoughts to
books@thomascook.com

● **Found a great bar, club, shop or must-see sight that we don't feature?**

● **Like to tip us off about any information that needs updating?**

● **Want to tell us what you love about this handy little guidebook and more importantly how we can make it even handier?**

Then here's your chance to tell all! Send us ideas, discoveries and recommendations today and then look out for your valuable input in the next edition of this title. As an extra 'thank you' from Thomas Cook Publishing, you'll be automatically entered into our exciting monthly prize draw.

Send an email to the above address (stating the book's title) or write to:
CitySpots Project Editor, Thomas Cook Publishing, PO Box 227,
The Thomas Cook Business Park, Unit 18, Coningsby Road,
Peterborough PE3 8SB, UK.